WINDOWS & SKYLIGHTS

BY THE EDITORS OF SUNSET BOOKS AND SUNSET MAGAZINE

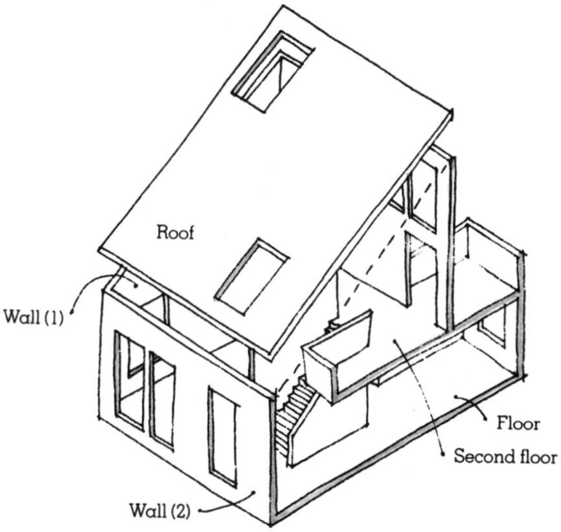

Roof

Wall (1)

Wall (2)

Floor

Second floor

LANE PUBLISHING CO.   MENLO PARK, CALIFORNIA

We gratefully acknowledge the help of the many professionals in the home improvement and building fields who shared their expertise with our editors. Special thanks go to the following individuals and companies: Acorn Structures, Inc., Randy Bettis, Harold Blomberg, Jerry Blomberg, Terry Burch, Paul Engelhart, Mike Felix, Arthur P. Jentoft, Lawrence Berkeley Laboratory, Paul Lombardi, Joey McHugh, Bruce McLean, Bob D. Moore, Richard E. Morgan, Bill O'Keefe, Lyndy Olstead, Pacific Skylight Company, Roland Pitschel, Diane Race, Peter C. Rodi, Pietro Rossi, Bob Shank, Joe Udovch, Von Dale Vaughn, Nyle Werthmann, Mike York, and William Zimmerman.

Cover: To take full advantage of spectacular view and admit maximum amount of light, upper-floor bedroom in remodeled city house combines windows and skylight. Bay window features double-hung sash and cleanly designed window seat. Pyramidal, tempered-glass skylight opens up ceiling; French doors extend vista, lead to small deck. Architect: Jennifer Clements. Photograph by Tom Wyatt. Cover design by JoAnn Masaoka.

Editor, Sunset Books: Elizabeth L. Hogan

Sixth printing January 1990

Photographers

Glenn Christiansen: 64 bottom left. **Jack McDowell:** 33, 35 bottom, 36 right, 38 right, 39 left & top right, 41 right, 43 bottom left & right, 44 left, 45 left, 47 top and bottom left, 48 left, 49 top & bottom, 50 top, 51, 53, 54 top, 55 top right & bottom, 56 right, 57 top, 58 right, 59 bottom right, 60 right, 64 top & bottom right. **Norman McGrath:** 50 bottom, 63 right. **Steve W. Marley:** 34 right, 35 top, 36 left, 37 top right & bottom, 38 left, 39 left, 40 bottom, 41 left, 42, 43 top, 44 right, 46 right, 47 right, 49 middle, 52, 54 bottom, 55 top left, 57 bottom right, 59 left, 60 left, 61, 62, 63 top & bottom left, 64 top left. **Rob Super:** 40 top, 57 bottom left. **Tom Wyatt:** 34 left, 37 top left, 39 bottom right, 45 right, 46 left, 48 right, 56 left, 58 left, 59 top right.

Coordinating Editor
Barbara J. Braasch

Research & Text
Don Rutherford
Sudha Irwin
Michael Scofield

Photo Editors
Scott Fitzgerrell
JoAnn Masaoka

Design
Joe di Chiarro

Illustrations
Suby T. Bowden
John D. Morrow
Jim Norris

CONTENTS

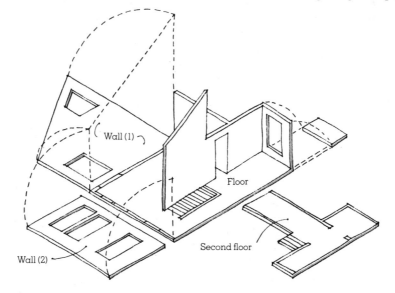

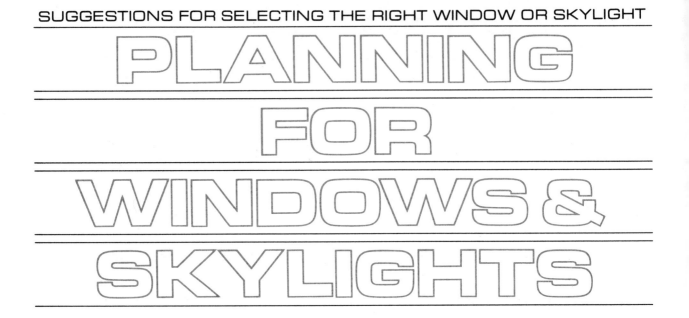

PLANNING FOR WINDOWS & SKYLIGHTS

The importance of admitting natural light to structures was no mystery even to the ancient Greeks and Romans. Not only did they appreciate the health-nurturing attributes of sunlight, but they also realized its hearth-warming quality. In Greece, entire cities were planned so homes, oriented to the south, could take advantage of the winter sun and reduce the dependence on precious charcoal for heat.

The Greeks, though, had no transparent window coverings; they shuttered their windows closed. Later, the Romans advanced Grecian solar architecture by using glass or mica to cover their windows and trap solar heat. In the middle of winter, wealthy Romans enjoyed fresh vegetables grown in south-facing greenhouses. Even the Roman bathhouses boasted large glazed windows to the south.

With today's dwindling fuel supplies and increasing fuel prices, we are once again beginning to appreciate the energy conservation potential of windows and skylights for heat, light, and ventilation. To realize their full potential, though, these openings have to be planned very carefully.

On the following pages, facts about lighting, as well as the other considerations you'll need to be aware of as you plan windows and skylights, are discussed. Understanding them will help you make informed decisions about these additions to your home.

WINDOW OR SKYLIGHT?

Clear or tinted, expansive or undersized, spectacular or unpretentious—windows and skylights come in an almost limitless assortment. To achieve the effect you want, you'll need to define your goals before you can begin planning. Only then can you decide where you want your openings and exactly which ones will work best for you.

Why do you want a window or skylight?

Perhaps it's a longing for beams of sunlight splashing across your breakfast table. Perhaps it's the desire to create a dramatic exterior design for your home. Or maybe it's the urgency to reduce fuel costs by admitting and trapping the sun's energy.

Whatever else windows and skylights are used for, their primary purpose is to admit light. One kind of lighting eases visual tasks like reading or sewing. Another kind creates a soothing, relaxed environment. Still a different lighting is required for dramatic effects.

Task lighting is the kind of light —natural or artificial—needed for writing, sewing, or other concentrated activity. This lighting requires a greater degree of contrast, measured not only in intensity, but also in quality and direction. A uniform level of light all around distracts the eye.

Plan task lighting so it comes from the right or the left of the viewer; you'll find reading and writing much easier if you sit with your side to the window, not facing it.

Too much contrast, though, will produce glare, which makes seeing difficult. A single, small window in the middle of a wall can be troublesome to look at if it's admitting direct sunlight.

Area lighting is the less concentrated, less intense light required for a hallway or living room. In such areas, lighting depends less on direct light than on reflected light from walls, ceiling, or mirrors.

When the walls and ceiling—as well as the light shaft of a skylight, if you have one—are painted in a light, nonglossy color, they become secondary light sources that spread the light evenly over an area.

This multidirectional lighting is perfect for setting a relaxed mood in a room; the reduced intensity of the light produces no glare or sharp contrasts.

Dramatic lighting effects depend on a beam of direct light— natural or artificial—focusing on art objects, plants, or a certain area. When the beam of light happens to be sunlight, usually from a skylight, its movement across the wall or floor provides interest and drama all day.

Access to light

If you're buiilding a new house or planning a major addition to an existing one, you can orient your rooms and design windows and skylights so they bring in light exactly where you want it. You're also free to choose between windows and skylights—or even to use a combination of the two.

But if you're not involved in major construction, your alternatives will be more restricted. Are the layout of your rooms and the orientation of your house such that you can have the morning light where

you want it? Even if your house is ideally oriented, is there a tall tree or a building obstructing the light?

Walk around your property; study the site and look for any obstructions that might prevent the light from falling where you want it. You'll also want to observe where the sun falls, both in the morning and the afternoon.

You'll have to opt for a skylight if, for reasons of security or privacy, the area you want to light cannot have a window; if you live in a row house where the only way to light middle rooms is from the top; or if obstructions on your site won't allow much light in through a window.

On the other hand, windows may be your only choice if you live in a two-story home.

Seasonal variations in sun angles

In winter, the sun travels in a low arc across the sky; during the summer months the arc is much higher. This allows the winter sun to penetrate deeper into a room through a south-facing window (north-facing in the southern hemisphere) than the summer sun (see below).

The amount of sunlight entering a skylight during the winter months depends on the angle of the skylight, the shape of the light shaft, and the latitude of your home.

(Continued on next page)

SEASONAL PATHS OF THE SUN

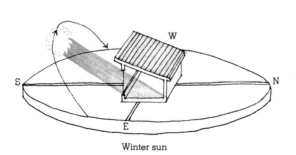

Winter sun

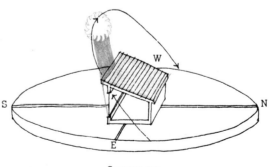

Summer sun

Height of sun's path above horizon changes during year. Light enters farther into room in winter, when path is low, than in summer, when path is high.

If you want heat gain in winter, you can have either a south-facing window or a properly designed skylight and light shaft (see page 18). But you can place a skylight so light reaches areas of a room that light from a window may not reach.

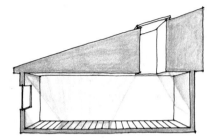

A skylight can give you a better distribution of light as well. These are important considerations if you intend to use the window or skylight for passive solar purposes.

In the summer, though, a south-facing skylight, unless shaded, will bring in more direct light and heat than a window; if the window has an overhang, the degree of penetration of the summer sun into your home is reduced even more (see page 30).

In a cold climate, a north-facing skylight may be better than a north-facing window, because an opening in the roof gives almost five times more light than an equivalent opening in the wall with approximately the same amount of heat loss.

Ventilation

Windows placed opposite one another at heights that let the incoming breeze wash around the room's occupants are the best way to ventilate and cool a room. When this positioning is not possible, the combination of a window and a venting or opening skylight works well. Since hot air rises, the venting skylight lets out warm air, and the cool breeze enters through the window.

For more information, see "Windows for ventilation" on page 9 and "Skylights for ventilation" on page 17.

Design considerations

A skylight brings in light and a view of the sky without taking up any wall space. A long, narrow diffusing skylight close to a wall can light art objects on that wall; a large clear or translucent north-facing skylight provides reliable, even light for an art studio.

On the other hand, a window, especially a bay or a bow, can add character and space to a room the way no skylight can. Add a window or greenhouse section to the south wall and you have created a great way to trap heat for your home. See page 10 for more on solar heating with windows.

CONSIDERATIONS IN WINDOW PLANNING

Not only do windows provide light, view, and ventilation, but they also can create a sense of space and act as passive solar devices to heat our homes. Whatever your primary goal, you'll want to be familiar with some basic principles that apply to each window function.

Windows for light

The orientation, placement, size, shape, and number of windows, as well as the colors in the room, will affect the intensity, distribution, and quality of the room's natural light.

Though you'll want all areas of the room to be lighted, it's wise to avoid absolutely uniform lighting —it will make the room look sterile and uninteresting. Also keep in mind that people tend to gravitate from darker to ligher areas, avoiding dark corners. The following pointers will help you achieve both deep penetration and good distribution of daylight within your room.

Window orientation. The orientation of your windows will have a significant effect on the amount of light they bring into your room. A south-facing window (north-facing

in the southern hemisphere) will let in the most light and is desirable in all but hot climates; a window oriented north provides soft, diffuse light. Light from east and west-facing windows requires careful management to control its intensity during the summer because of the low sun angles in the morning and late afternoon.

When you're figuring the size of the window, remember that useful light from a window penetrates not more than 2½ times the height of the window. The only way to overcome this limitation is with clerestory windows deep in the room (see page 13), a skylight, or additional windows or other walls.

Number and shape of windows. Whether your wall space is severely limited or you're able to design with abandon, you'll want to understand the following principles of how the shape and number of windows affect light distribution.

● One large window or several small ones grouped together may give more even, glare-free light than separate small windows.

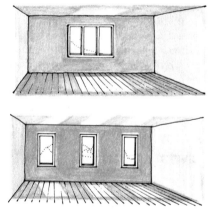

● Windows in more than one wall provide more pleasant and uniform distribution of light than windows in a single wall. You'll also have good illumination over a larger portion of the day.

● Short, wide windows create a broad, shallow distribution of light; tall, narrow windows provide a thin, deep distribution. But if a tall, narrow window is situated near a light-colored wall, its effectiveness is enhanced because the wall reflecting the light becomes a secondary light source. To reduce the glare from a tall, narrow window in an east or west-facing wall, place the window high on the wall to avoid a direct view of the sun; or screen the window on the outside.

Wide window creates broad pattern.

Narrow window creates thin pattern.

Wall adjoining window reflects light.

High window creates deep pattern.

Reflected light. Exterior surfaces adjacent to a window reflect light to varying degrees and can affect the amount of light entering a window.

Likewise, reflections from interior surfaces affect the intensity and distribution of light within the room. A white wall reflects as much as 90 percent of the light. Medium tones, such as tan, rose, light blue, green, and gray, reflect 30 to 50 percent. Dark colors and dark woods reflect less than 15 percent of the light.

Maximizing light. Mount draperies, shades, and other window coverings so they clear the glass areas completely when they're open, and you won't lose any light from those windows.

Screens can absorb as much as 50 percent of available light; to avoid losing light, use them sparingly, and then only over the opening parts of the windows. Windows with tinted glass will reduce glare.

Windows for view

Being able to look out of a window is as important to us as receiving light and air through them. Windows connect us to the environment, enhance our sense of space, and satisfy our curiosity.

You'll want to determine the placement and size of your window by what you will see from it. Just as the framing brings out the best in an oil painting, so it is with a view, whether it's a panorama of the mountains or a glimpse into a small intimate garden.

Selecting the right window. If a spectacular view demands a large picture window, consider breaking up the expanse of glass with muntins (see page 11). The small panes will create a multitude of framed views, enhancing your relationship with the outside and retaining your sense of security and shelter.

Some architects recommend several smaller windows instead of one large window; this allows people to catch glimpses of the view as they move around the house. The view becomes a little less overwhelming and doesn't lose its attraction as readily as if it's seen in its entirety from a sitting area.

Try to avoid or minimize large obstructions in the line of sight. Horizontal divisions, especially more than 4 inches wide, are undesirable; vertical ones don't create so much of a problem. And remember that screens can interfere with a clear view; if you don't need ventilation, consider fixed glass.

Window placement. Situate the windows in your room where they'll provide the best possible view of the outside; avoid windows that look out on a wall or a fence.

Even if your home fronts on a busy street, you can satisfy your family's curiosity about what's going on by designing a second-story window or a high first-floor window so passersby can't look in. If noise is a problem, double glazing (see page 25) can reduce it.

When you're planning the height of the window sill, take into account not only the view, but also the room's function and furniture arrangement. Ideally, the sill should be below eye level. But in a kitchen, you may want the sill above the level of the counter; in a dining room, at about the level of the table; and in a bedroom, at about 4 feet from the floor (see page 9).

If you have a patio, deck, or garden outside your bedroom, consider placing the sill 10 to 14 inches from the floor. Then you'll be able to see outside without craning your neck above a high sill. The same sill height works in a living room and allows you and your guests to view the outdoors from a sitting position (see drawing on page 9). Most building codes require the use of tempered glass within 18 inches of the floor.

When your're planning to add a window or skylight, a cardboard model of your room is an invaluable tool. Without actually cutting any holes in the walls or roof of your home, you can check the light and view from a proposed window or analyze the quality and amount of light you'll gain from a skylight.

Building a model adequate for studying the placement and size of a proposed window or skylight is simple and requires only several hours of time and a few dollars for materials.

Materials and tools for the model

Before buying any materials, measure your room's floor, walls, and ceiling, and note the size and location of existing windows and skylights. Unless the roof is flat, you'll need to measure the roof and its slope. To keep track of your measurements, make a sketch of each area, marking all of the dimensions. You'll also need to know the dimensions of the window or skylight you're planning to install.

Use a scale of ½ inch or 1 inch per foot. Then estimate the amount of material you'll need for the model.

Buy enough extra material to make several versions of the wall or ceiling where you intend to put the window or skylight.

Make the model from corrugated cardboard, cardboard or plastic-foam mounting board (available at art supply stores), or balsa wood (available at hobby stores). Using plastic-foam mounting board or balsa wood allows you to glue the cutouts back into the walls or ceiling if you change your mind.

You'll also need white glue, straight pins, a ruler, a square, a pencil, and a sharp knife.

Building the model

Choose a flat surface to work on; you may want to protect it with a panel of plywood or hardboard. Using the scale you have chosen, draw the floor plan, walls, ceiling, and roof on the building material. Mark all existing and proposed openings.

Cut the floor, walls, ceiling, and roof; then cut the window, door, and skylight openings.

With the floor plan as your guide, glue or pin walls to the floor and to each other; then glue the ceiling and the roof. You may want to cut and glue light shaft walls to the open-

ing edges of the skylight before attaching the roof to the walls. If you want to be able to make changes, use the glue sparingly so you can remove and replace walls easily.

How to use the model

To see how your new skylight or window will alter the light in your home, place your model in direct sunlight, facing in the same direction as your house. Use small plants to simulate any trees that cast shadows on your house.

Observe the model at different times of day—morning, noon, afternoon, and evening—and study the quality and intensity of the changing light. To study the effect of sunlight at different times of the year, you can tilt the model to simulate the change in the height of the sun during the year. Place the model on a table outside the room, and study the view through the proposed window.

Move, reduce, or enlarge the opening for proposed window or skylight until you get the effect you want. You may even want to change an existing window. Once you're satisfied, you'll be much more confident about cutting holes in the walls or roof of your home.

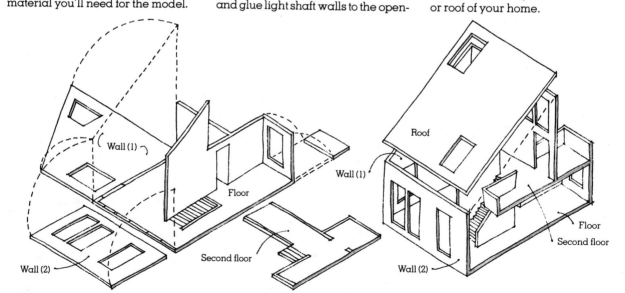

Windows for ventilation

Air moves because of a difference in temperature or pressure. Warm air rises; in a single-story house, warm air venting through an open skylight creates an air flow and pulls air in through an open window.

It's the pressure difference, though, that mainly influences air flow—from high pressure to low. When wind hits the wall of a house, air pressure rises along that wall; on the opposite side of the house where there's protection from the wind, air pressure drops. Windows in these two walls optimize air movement; air coming in through one window and exiting through the window on the opposite wall creates cross ventilation, a relief on warm summer nights. This positioning is most effective in north and south walls.

Study seasonal wind patterns around your house, and, if you can, place windows to take advantage of the prevailing breezes.

In summer, some of the cooling effect of air depends on its speed. To accelerate the flow of air through an area, make the windows through which air exits larger than the ones through which it enters. Take a look outside for any obstructions that can slow the movement of air. Even furniture or room partitions can reduce air flow.

Air currents through a house provide the greatest comfort when they flow at the level of the occupants. If possible, place windows low in the wall, unless you use awnings or jalousie windows which can direct air flow downward (see page 12). Also, keeping windows away from corners maximizes air movement.

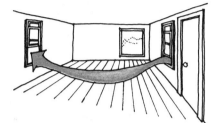

For best cooling effect, exit window should be opened wider than entry.

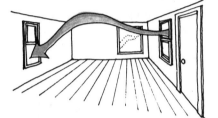

With top sash of entry window open, cooling air flows above occupants.

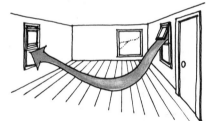

Awning entry window directs air downward toward open exit window.

All but swinging windows open only 50 percent and cannot change air direction, so place them directly in front of the area through which you want air to move. Casements, awnings, and other swinging windows give you a 100 percent opening; they can be used to direct air sideways, upwards, or downwards.

Windows for appearance

If you're adding or replacing windows in an existing structure, you'll want to pay particular attention to their style; the type, size, and placement of windows you choose will affect not only their performance, but also the interior and exterior design of your home.

You'll want to select windows that match your home's general style. Before adding or replacing a window, stand outside your house and study the arrangement of the existing windows. Draw plans to see how the new addition will affect the building's exterior appearance. If the new window has to be a different size than the existing ones, plan it so the house has a balanced appearance.

Windows and privacy

Windows provide light, view, and ventilation, but they also allow others to see inside your home. In addition to curtains, draperies, and shades for privacy protection, you

WINDOW PLACEMENT

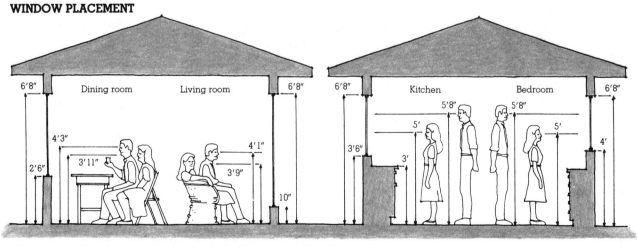

Plan your windows for easy viewing from standing or seated position.

can plant shrubs or trees outside your windows. Glazing windows wholly or partially with translucent glass is another way to prevent intrusion on your privacy.

Windows and solar heating

For windows to admit the maximum amount of the sun's heat, they must face south (north in the southern hemisphere) or within 20° east or west of true south. This orientation is essential for catching the winter sun (see page 5).

When the sun's direct rays enter a house, their radiant energy or heat is trapped inside, but only for the time the sunlight is present. When the sun goes down, interior heat is transmitted out through the glass to the colder environment. To retard this heat loss, you can install double glazing (see page 25) or cover the window with insulating material (see page 27). In cold climates, you may want to do both.

In a passive solar heating system, you can store the heat by letting the sunlight fall on a material, such as brick, masonry, concrete, or water, that will absorb and store the heat; after sundown, the material slowly releases its heat into the surrounding environment, keeping the house interior warm (see above right). When this method is used in conjunction with movable window insulation, we derive the greatest benefit from the sun's heat.

Both elements—the south-facing glass to admit the sun's radiation and a thermal mass to absorb the radiation and later release heat —are the basis of a passive solar system. You'll want to consider some other points when using windows as passive solar devices.

• South-facing windows can provide a net positive energy balance, losing less heat than they gain, if they are both double or triple glazed and covered with insulating material at night.

• Clear glazing gives the maximum amount of light and heat for the area covered.

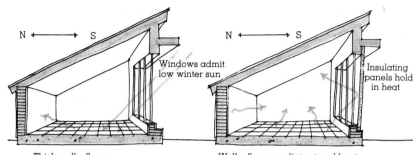

Thick walls, floor absorb and store sun's heat

Walls, floor reradiate stored heat

• The south-facing window should not be obstructed between 9 A.M. and 3 P.M. because almost 95 percent of the low winter sun is intercepted between those hours.

• Recessing windows back from the outside wall will reduce air movement against them, reducing air infiltration. Splaying that recessed opening will increase the

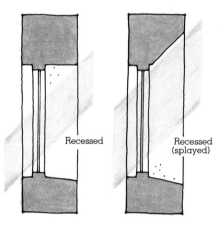

Recessed

Recessed (splayed)

amount of direct sunlight coming through in winter, but it will also reduce shading in summer.

• A south-facing window's height will limit how far from the window the thermal mass can be placed—generally only as far as 2½ times the window's height, since this is how far the direct sunlight will penetrate.

You'll find more information on controlling heat in the chapter beginning on page 24. For more details on passive solar systems, see the *Sunset* book *Homeowner's Guide to Solar Heating & Cooling*.

CHOOSING YOUR WINDOWS

Never has there been a greater variety of windows from which to choose. They come in all shapes, sizes, and designs, with different kinds of window materials, glazing (see page 16), and weatherstripping (see page 93).

How do you select the window that's right for you? You'll want to consider several criteria—your budget, the existing windows and the architectural style of your home, and your needs. Does the window give you the light, ventilation, or view that you want? Is it well insulated and weatherproof? Will it be easy to operate and maintain? Can you install it yourself?

In the following pages, we discuss the basic window styles and situations that call for special designs. The different glazings and window materials you can choose from are also covered.

Basic window styles

Study the windows in your home and in the houses in your neighborhood. At first glance, the windows may all look very different because of the variety of sizes, shapes, and muntin arrangements. But it's likely that all the windows fall into four basic categories— sliding, swinging, fixed, or rotary (see illustration on page 12).

Sliding windows have movable sashes that slide in either horizontal or vertical tracks. These windows—double-hung, vertical sliding, and horizontal sliding—are good for harsh climates since sliding sashes generally seal more tightly than swinging sashes. But they're not as suitable for ventilation because only half the window can be opened at a time, and a breeze cannot be directed to different areas of the room.

Double-hung windows, the most widely used of all styles, have two sashes—an upper, or outside, sash that moves down and a lower, or inside, sash that moves up in grooves in the frame. The sash movements and positions are controlled by springs, by weights, or by friction devices. Some sashes are removable or rotatable, helpful for window cleaning.

A double-hung window is a good choice for rooms that open onto porches or walkways, since it won't interfere with people passing by. But reaching the top sash may be difficult if the window is located above the kitchen sink or behind a large piece of furniture. Also, when you want to enjoy a view, the horizontal division in this window may interfere with your line of vision.

Vertical sliding or single-hung windows are made just like the double-hung ones, except only one sash—usually the lower one—

moves. The upper sash is usually stationary.

Horizontal sliding windows, as the name suggests, have sashes that slide horizontally in metal or plastic tracks. In the double-sliding variety, both sashes move; in the single-sliding type, one is fixed.

Most models have at least one removable sash, so unless the sashes are too large to handle, you can easily wash them.

Sliding doors are larger versions of this window (see page 84).

Swinging windows include casements with sashes that swing out, and hoppers and awning windows with outward or inward-swinging sashes. Because swinging windows are usually easy to operate, you can place them in hard-to-reach areas. But you may not want to install casements or awnings where people outside can bump into the open sashes.

Casement windows, hung singly or in pairs, have sashes that swing outward. The modern ones are operated with a crank. If on a large window the crank pushes only the lower part of a sash, it can eventually distort the sash and prevent a tight closure.

A casement is an excellent choice for summer ventilation; the window can be opened all the way, and the outswinging sashes can scoop in air not blowing directly into the window.

Most casements available today have an arm's width of space between the opened sash and the frame; this allows you to clean the outside of the sash from the inside.

Awning windows pivot at the top and may be purchased with outward or inward-swinging sashes. The window is usually operated with a crank. Check to make sure that the hinges are sturdy and allow both sides of the sash to move equally; this will prevent twisting the sash.

Since top-hinged windows direct air downward, they're best placed high in the wall for ventilation purposes. They're particularly suited to basement installations.

You can adjust the sash so rain is kept out but air let in. Depending on the angle of the open sash, an awning can also direct air upward into a room.

Hopper windows, the reverse of awning windows, pivot at the bottom and open inward. Since these windows can direct air upward only, they should be placed

WINDOW ANATOMY

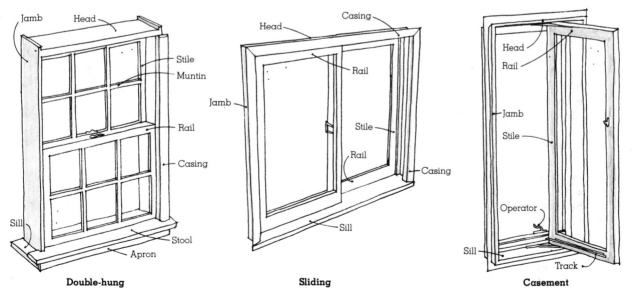

Double-hung

Sliding

Casement

Awning

Jalousie

Double-hung

Sliding

Casement

Hopper

Rotary

Fixed

low in a wall. You won't be able to use the space directly in front of them, but you will find hoppers easy to operate and wash.

Jalousie windows are made of a number of horizontal glass slats set in metal clips. A crank opens and closes the slats in unison. These windows operate much like awning windows (especially stacked units), but the glass slats don't protrude as far when they're opened as an awning sash.

Because the slats don't seal completely when closed, the jalousie is more suitable for warm climates and for areas that don't need to be heated or air-conditioned.

Fixed windows, often called picture windows, can be used alone or in combination with windows with movable sashes. Traditionally glazed with a single large pane of glass to take advantage of a view,

fixed windows are now available with a variety of muntin arrangements which are easily removable to facilitate cleaning.

Rotary windows, designed in Europe, have sashes that rotate on pivots on each side of the frame. Some are designed to be installed in sloping surfaces, such as the roof above a finished attic; others can be used in walls. But in all of them, the rotating sash permits easy cleaning and a range of ventilation angles to direct air straight in, upward, or downward. Almost all of them can be opened to allow some air movement and still keep the rain out.

Some rotating windows operate with a crank that controls the pivots at the sides of the sash; others have a control bar at the top of the sash. As the sash rotates, the bottom swings out much farther than the top swings in, allowing use of the space near the window.

Windows for special situations

When your turn-of-the-century home demands a fixed-glass window with a semicircular top, or your A-frame in the country requires a triangular window, you may need to have a window custom-built. But you'll find an impressive collection of creative window styles that you can obtain ready-made.

Your architect and your local window dealers can help you get the window you want. The choices are limited only by your imagination. For ideas on using windows inventively, see page 32.

Specially designed windows can brighten a dark interior, provide light and warmth for an indoor garden, or create an intimate seat where you can curl up with a book.

A half-circle frame with fixed glass looks dramatic above a

square or rectangular picture window; a round or octagonal window with translucent or stained glass is striking in a hallway, stairwell, or bathroom (see right). When a front entrance leads into a dark hallway, you can illuminate the interior with a vertical strip of windows on one or both sides of the door.

In any room where you spend time during the day, try to have an area where you can see out comfortably. An alcove or bay window with a window seat or a large window with a low sill can be a relaxing and attractive addition.

If the windows will face a patio, garden, or cooling breezes, be sure they can open wide. This will allow fresh air to flow into the room and permit you to enjoy the sights and sounds outside. Make these windows easily accessible and low to the floor, even all the way to the floor like French doors.

Window seats are great for relaxing or reading, but only if they're comfortable. Before you build one, put an armchair or sofa where you want the window seat and try it out. If the chair or sofa isn't comfortable, try another. When you're satisfied, build the seat as wide and as well padded as the chair or sofa for built-in comfort.

Bay windows and their variations, bows, oriels (cantilevered bows), and popouts, project from the wall, adding space to the interior, providing a place to enjoy the outside, and enhancing the view.

A bay window has a fixed center window parallel to the wall

SPECIAL WINDOWS

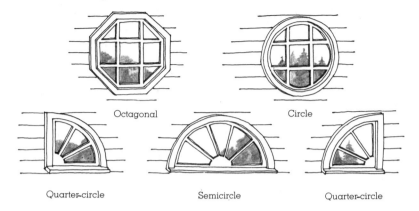

Octagonal   Circle

Quarter-circle   Semicircle   Quarter-circle

flanked by two opening windows—casements or double-hung—attached at an angle.

A bow window projects like a bay, but has more than three sections in it, all of which may be opening. A bow window's sections are set at gentle angles, giving the window a curved appearance.

Oriels are bays that project from the upper story of a house and are almost always supported by brackets.

Popouts are custom-designed windows installed in sections that cantilever from the wall of the house. Somewhat similar to bays, they vary greatly in their design depending on the need they serve. Sometimes, the popouts reach to the roof.

Clerestory windows, also known as "ribbon windows," are a set of windows that run along the top of a wall near the ceiling. The windows often have fixed glass, though some

have sliding or hinged sashes.

Clerestory windows are ideal for admitting natural light and solar

heat deep into a space without sacrificing privacy.

Cathedral and multistory windows both have large expanses of glass. In a cathedral window, the glass is fixed and the window is set above a sliding or picture window in a room with a very high ceiling. Admitting extra light and view, the window generally follows the slope of the roof and, depending on its size, may have vertical divisions.

As the name implies, multistory windows extend from the ground floor to the floors above; the glass can be fixed or opening.

In homes where cathedral or multistory windows are used, rooms on the upper floors generally have openings facing them so they can share the light and view.

PROJECTING WINDOWS

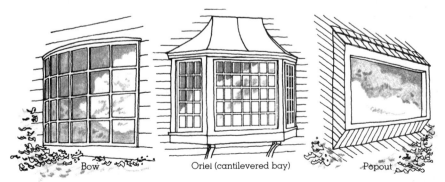

Bow   Oriel (cantilevered bay)   Popout

Interior windows are openings on inside walls that allow rooms to share light and view, add a sense of space, and let people communicate with each other. If privacy is desired, the opening can be closed off with shutters, blinds, or an operable sash of translucent glass.

Greenhouse windows, made of metal or wood, are relatively small baylike windows designed for growing plants. They come with shelves for pots and planters and are usually made to fit standard-size window openings. Some have opening sides or tops for ventilation.

They're favorite additions in kitchens and bathrooms, where the moisture, together with the heat and light coming in through the window, produces thriving plants.

Solariums, sunrooms, and greenhouse sections all have walls of glass. Solariums and sunrooms are porches or rooms that usually face south, taking advantage of the sun's warmth. They may be part of the original house or added on later (see page 58).

Both the walls and the roof of a greenhouse section are made of glass. A greenhouse section forming the wall and roof of a living area in your home provides a bright, cheery environment. When combined with a thermal mass, a south-facing greenhouse wall becomes a passive solar device that helps to heat your house in winter. But you'll need to provide shading in the summer to control unwanted solar gain.

Even when they're not used as passive solar devices, these sunny enclosures add usable space to a house and fresh vegetables and flowers to the table even in the middle of winter.

Window materials

Windows may be wood, aluminum, steel, or vinyl, or, for improved weathering and insulation, a combination of these materials. Though windows with better weather protection are more expensive, they can pay off in energy savings.

Wood windows are warm, traditional, and esthetically pleasing. Because it's a good insulator, wood does not become cold like metal and glass, so the moisture in the warm interior air doesn't condense on it. But since wood is subject to shrinkage and swelling, it will warp and rot in time unless protected by preservatives and paint.

Most available wood windows are primed or treated with chemicals to reduce the effects of weathering. Some manufacturers cover the wood with vinyl, others with colored aluminum for better weather protection and reduced maintenance.

Aluminum windows, more durable than wood, are also thinner, lighter, and easier to handle. But aluminum is a poor insulator, so in cold weather some heat is lost through the metal; also, condensation can form on the inside of the sash.

Several manufacturers solve these problems by insulating the aluminum with wood or plastic foam. This provides a thermal break between the inner and outer surfaces of the sash and frame that reduces heat loss and eliminates condensation.

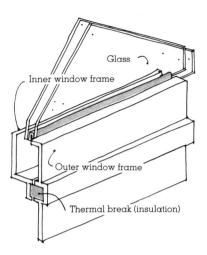

Glass
Inner window frame
Outer window frame
Thermal break (insulation)

Aluminum windows are available in clear satin finish, baked enamel finish in several colors, or clear or bronze-anodized finish (anodization is a process that covers a metal electrolytically with a protective oxide). All but the satin finish help protect the aluminum sash from corrosion and eliminate the need for maintenance. They are not recommended, though, for use near the ocean, where the salt spray can be highly corrosive.

Steel windows are now used more often in commercial buildings than in homes. These windows are generally more expensive than either wood or aluminum ones. Though steel is somewhat less conductive thermally than aluminum, it too allows condensation in the absence of a thermal break. It also rusts easily unless primed and painted. Stainless steel weathers better than ordinary steel, but it's very expensive and not readily available for residential use.

Because steel is stronger than both aluminum and wood, steel windows have very thin frame members that look quite attractive. But their extra cost prevents most people from using them in homes, except as replacement windows to match older existing ones.

Vinyl windows, relative newcomers to the marketplace, have members extruded from high impact-resistant, rigid polyvinyl

(Continued on page 16)

Popular from the 1920s through the 1950s, glass blocks are staging a comeback in the early '80s. Think of glass blocks as translucent or transparent bricks that soften light by diffusing it, eliminating glare. You can use them wherever you don't have to have ventilation but want to bring in light—both on the exterior and in the interior of your home.

Why the renewed interest in glass blocks?

Made by fusing two halves of pressed glass together, creating a partial vacuum inside, glass blocks have the same insulating value as double glazing glass or a 12-inch-thick concrete wall.

Because glass blocks can transmit up to 80 percent of the available daylight, they're ideal for bathrooms where you want both light and privacy, and for house plants, which thrive in the filtered light. Glass block windows in an entry or over a kitchen counter can provide natural light, yet preserve security.

In a room heated to 70°F/21C° with 40 percent humidity, glass blocks remain free of obscuring condensation until the outside temperature drops to 24°F below zero

(−31°C); under similar conditions, condensation would form at 30°F/−2°C on a single-glazed window. Because glass blocks are installed without a sash, there's no metal to rust and no wood to rot; nothing needs to be puttied, caulked, or painted.

Mortared in place, the glass blocks are thick and virtually impenetrable. They form a barrier to intruders, reduce noise by an average of 40 decibels, and prevent dust and dirt from entering your house. Since a glass block window is leakproof, it may be the solution to the problem of water seepage through a basement window. See below and pages 53 and 57 for examples of the use of glass blocks.

Maintenance is simple: just clean the inside surface with a cloth dampened with window cleaner and wash the outside surface with a hose.

Obtaining glass blocks

You can buy 3 or 4-inch-thick square glass blocks in many sizes; rectangular blocks are available in a more limited selection. Each block weighs 4 pounds or more, depending on its size. Textures range from smooth to

rippled, bubbly, crosshatched, or faceted. Though untinted glass is most common, amber and gray tints are also available; for sun control, you can use bronze or gray-surfaced solar reflective glass. Prism edges molded into the surface of some blocks turn daylight into color.

One manufacturer makes preassembled glass block panels that are available with louvered ventilators.

To locate glass block, look in the Yellow Pages of your telephone directory under "Glass—Block, Structural, Etc." You may be able to special-order the blocks through a regular glass dealer. It's possible that you can even find some glass blocks in salvage yards.

Doing the work yourself

Laying glass blocks is a lot like laying bricks, but there are some special details you need to know for proper installation. For instructions, consult a manufacturer or supplier.

You also need to check your local building code for construction requirements for glass blocks. Once you know what's involved, you'll be able to decide whether or not you can do the work yourself.

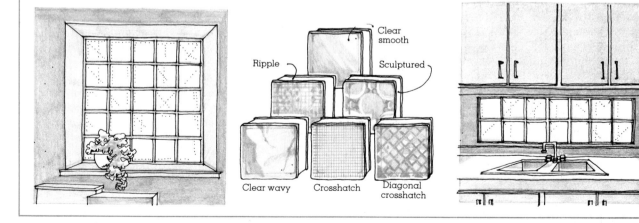

Clear smooth

Ripple

Sculptured

Clear wavy

Crosshatch

Diagonal crosshatch

. . . Continued from page 14

chloride. Vinyl has excellent weathering resistance and is maintenance free. When the material is fabricated into hollow shapes for window members, it has excellent resistance to heat loss, so there's virtually no condensation.

Vinyl windows are available in several different colors. Because the color is integral with the vinyl, you don't have to paint vinyl windows.

Window glazing materials

Though we think of glass as the traditional glazing material for windows, plastic glazing is increasing in popularity. With either glass or plastic, you have many choices for appearance, color, solar benefit, insulating qualities, and light transmission.

Glass that's used for panes in windows and doors is typically single or double strength and ⅛ inch thick or less. In small picture windows and glass doors, the glass is usually ¼ inch thick, though the larger the window, the thicker the glass must be. Let a professional determine the thickness required for a large window; if the glass isn't thick enough, strong winds may shatter it.

Insulating glass is an assembly of two or three panes of glass separated by moisture-free air space. A drying agent in the frame surrounding the glass keeps the air dry; this reduces the possibility of condensation—or ice in freezing climates—forming, obscuring the view and reducing the insulating qualities. Insulating glass also acts as soundproofing.

Double-glazed glass (two panes) has a 95 percent higher resistance to heat flow than single glazing. In a very cold climate, you may want to consider a triple-glazed insulating window, which has a 45 percent higher resistance to heat flow than double glazing.

Whether insulating glass will reduce your heating and cooling costs enough to warrant the added expense depends on a number of factors and should be evaluated by an architect, heating engineer, or glass specialist.

Insulating glass is available in a range of standard sizes; you also have a choice of tinted or coated glass (see below).

Some manufacturers offer double glazing with transparent insulation between the panes. This allows solar radiation to enter, but blocks heat passage out from the room through the window.

Tinted and coated glass reduce the amount of light, glare, and heat from the sun (see drawing on page 30). Colors available include blue, green, gray, silver, bronze, and gold.

The color in tinted glass runs through the material, making the glass transparent. Coated glass has a film on one side that reflects light and heat; from the outside, the window looks like a mirror, which adds to your privacy. Care must be used when cleaning coated glass to avoid damaging the coating (see page 30).

If you're concerned about bleaching the color from fabrics and other materials, you may want to use glass that filters out the ultraviolet light in sunshine.

Textured glass, available in a number of patterns and colors, is used for light with privacy and for decorative purposes. Light passing through the glass can create pleasing patterns of sunlight on your walls and floor.

Safety glass may be required by local building codes for certain situations and is always a good choice where a person could walk into a door or window.

Safety glass is available tempered, laminated, or wire reinforced. Tempered glass is heat-treated during the manufacturing process after it's cut to size to in-

crease its strength and resistance to shattering. Laminated glass consists of a sheet of plastic laminated between two panes of glass. Because it's not very attractive, wire-reinforced glass is seldom used in homes.

Plastic is a fairly new material for glazing. Though marketed under a number of trade names, it's usually made of either acrylic or polycarbonate (see page 21). Since the differences between the two materials are quite subtle, you'll probably base your choice on other characteristics—availability, color, texture, and light and heat transmission.

Plastic varies in thickness from ⅛ inch to ½ inch. As with glass, a larger area requires thicker material. Plastic glazing is lighter and more shatter-resistant than glass, but it scratches easily and must be cleaned with care.

Molding plastic into complex shapes and curves for skylights and bubble windows is done at the factory. Unlike glass, it can even be shaped on the job for custom installation.

With plastic, you can choose from a number of textured surfaces and even more colors than with glass. In addition to clear plastic, you may select from solar bronze and gray, white, translucent, and a number of transparent and semiopaque colors. Special plastics that transmit or absorb ultraviolet light are available also.

Though plastics are not factory-made into double and triple-thick insulating windows, you can double and triple glaze on the job, but you may have to contend with condensation between the panes later on. You can also purchase clear, translucent white, or bronze plastic insulating panels; these are molded from two sheets of plastic connected by internal ribs. Because of the internal ribs, vision through the clear material is impaired. The panel's resistance to heat loss, though, is slightly better than double-glazed insulating glass.

CONSIDERATIONS IN SKYLIGHT PLANNING

A skylight adds light, view, and, in some cases, ventilation without affecting privacy or taking up any wall space. With a skylight, you can create an indoor garden and enhance the interior design of your room. When properly oriented to take advantage of the sun's heat and insulated, a skylight can also warm your house in winter.

Planning constraints. Whatever your goal, you'll need to take into account certain limitations before you can begin planning a skylight.

• If there's an attic or crawl space between the ceiling and the

roof, you must have a light shaft to direct the light through the attic to the room below.

• The longer the light shaft, the larger the skylight must be to achieve the same level of lighting on a given area. Even if the shaft is light colored, some light will be lost.

• Structural limitations, such as roof members or proximity to a weight-bearing wall, may prevent you from placing the skylight where you want it. If you have easy access to your attic, check for potential problems in placement (see page 99).

Skylights for light

All skylights bring in light, but the quality and quantity of illumination are affected by their orientation and glazing. A south-facing skylight (north-facing in the southern hemisphere) with clear glazing brings in a great amount of light and heat, but it may produce glare. Use it for creating a mood or providing visual interest.

For uniform, soft lighting, use a north-facing skylight or one with

either translucent glazing or a diffusing panel at the ceiling level (see page 109).

If you want a skylight for an indoor garden, your choice will depend on the kind of plants you want to grow. A clear unit is best for plants that need direct sunlight. But remember that sunbeams keep moving throughout the day—track the sun's motion and plant accordingly. For most other types of plants that don't require direct light, a skylight with translucent glazing works well.

Skylights for view

Skylights with clear or tinted glazing allow you to enjoy the view overhead. Bronze or gray-tinted glazing produces less glare and heat than a clear unit.

When you're considering skylight placement, remember that though a view of the trees might be pleasant, putting your unit directly under a tree can present problems, since dirt and debris will collect on it.

Skylights for ventilation

For ventilation purposes, you will obviously select a unit that opens. These units work well in bathrooms and kitchens, or in any other area in which you need ventilation.

You'll also appreciate a venting unit if you live in a warm climate or have a flat-roofed house; when combined with a few open windows, opening the skylight at night will allow hot air to escape, cooling down your house.

Skylights and solar heating

When skylights, like windows, are oriented south (north in the southern hemisphere) or within 20° east or west of true south, they'll admit the maximum amount of the sun's heat in winter. For optimum solar gain, you'll want to tilt the skylight toward the south at an angle of the area's latitude plus 15°.

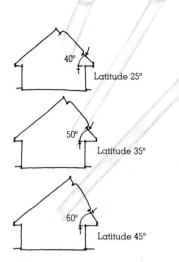

You can do this easily if you have a pitched roof. But if your roof is flat and you desire winter heat gain, plan on mounting a reflector on the north side of the installation so the low-angle sun is directed through the skylight.

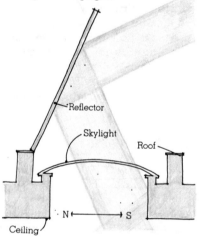

Clear glazing admits the maximum amount of light and heat for the area covered. As an added bonus, several states consider a south-facing skylight with clear glazing as a passive solar device and allow tax credits for its installation.

If your skylight is sizable, you may want to shade it either from the inside or from the outside to reduce unwanted solar gain in summer (see page 31).

Translucent glazing reduces glare and also reduces solar gain. So does tinted glazing; it cuts down both light transmission and solar radiation to a considerable degree.

Skylight sizing considerations

How large a skylight you get will depend not only on the depth and shape of the light shaft, but also on the size of the area you want to light or heat and the reflection of the surfaces in that area.

Light shafts. You'll need a light shaft—either straight, angled, or splayed—if there's a space between the roof and the ceiling (see below). In a straight light shaft, the skylight sits directly above the ceiling opening. The skylight is positioned off to one side of the ceiling opening in an angled light shaft. In a splayed light shaft, the ceiling opening is larger than the roof opening; the skylight can sit above or to the side of the ceiling opening.

Sizing principles. A general rule of thumb for determining skylight area is to figure on 1 square foot of skylight area for every 20 square feet of floor space. For example, if your room area is 100 square feet, your skylight area will be 5 square feet.

TYPES OF SHAFTS

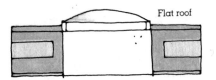

Flat roof

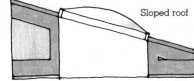

Sloped roof

Straight

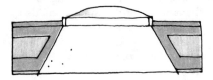

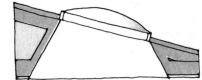

Splayed

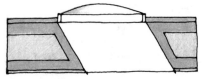

Angled

Though you can use any size skylight with any rafter spacing, most prefabricated units are designed to fit a roof with either 16 or 24-inch rafter spacing, or a multiple of these spacings; this makes installation easier and more economical.

The deeper your light shaft and the higher your ceiling, the larger your skylight will have to be to provide the desired amount of light. But you can bring in the same amount of light with a smaller skylight if you use a light shaft splayed between 30° and 60°.

Light-colored ceiling, walls, light shaft, and furnishings reflect more light, requiring a smaller glazing area for a given lighting requirement.

CHOOSING YOUR SKYLIGHT

You can buy a prefabricated skylight, have one specially made for your needs, or, if you have the necessary expertise, build one yourself.

Should you feel inclined to build your own because the standard skylights don't fully meet your needs, be aware of the problems lying in wait. Before undertaking the task, you'll need to know the basics of roof construction and the characteristics of the materials used for the skylight.

Failure to properly design, build, or install the skylight can allow wind-driven rain, melting ice, or condensation on the inner surface of the skylight to damage your walls and drip down on you. Skylights have even been known to collapse under heavy snow loads. Another problem you can encounter is heat loss through the skylight in winter and an undesirable buildup of heat during the summer.

If you do want to build your own skylight, the best way to avoid these pitfalls is to have an architect or other professional design the project.

Prefabricated skylights

The most economical, and usually the most reliable, choice for your skylight is a prefabricated unit. Manufacturers offer skylights in a variety of shapes, sizes, and glazings, and in both fixed and opening designs.

Skylight shapes and sizes. Skylights range in shape from square to circular (see page 20). They may be flat, domed, or pyramidal, and can vary in size from one small enough to fit between two rafters to a skylight large enough to roof a small room. Several skylights can even be combined to form one large unit.

If you live in snow country, avoid flat skylights; domed and pyramidal shapes are better for supporting snow loads.

Skylights with flat surfaces can be glazed with glass or plastic. Domed skylights are always glazed with some type of plastic, a material that molds easily into complex shapes. See page 21 for more information on skylight glazing.

(Continued on page 20)

Elegant, nostalgic, and colorful, stained glass can turn a window into a work of art. With its combinations of hues and patterns and with the changing light of day, stained glass can liven up any room. Even after dark, you can turn on the room lights and enjoy the translucent tapestry of stained glass from your patio or garden.

Depending on its design, a stained glass window can also provide privacy both at night and during the day.

Stained glass panels

Traditionally, an artist or artisan made a stained glass panel by fitting pieces of glass into channels in lead strips, soldering the strips together at their corners, and strengthening and waterproofing the seams with putty. A more recently developed technique involves wrapping copper foil tape around the edges of each piece of glass, fitting the pieces together, and soldering the seams.

The glass used in the panels can be mineral hued, painted, clear, sandblasted, or mirrored. Textures can vary from smooth to rough, rippled, or knobby. Beveled edges on clear pieces can break white light into rainbows.

To build your own stained glass panel, look for classes given by schools, museums, or private studios; materials are available in supply centers (look under "Glass—Stained & Leaded" in the Yellow Pages of your telephone directory). You can buy completed assembled panels, new or old, in supply centers, flea markets, and antique shops. Or for a stained glass panel custom-made to your own specifications, you can hire a professional to design and construct one.

Design pointers

Whether you intend to make a panel yourself or buy one, consider the effect you want the stained glass to have, the size and color scheme of the room, the direction the panel will face, and the amount of outdoor view you'd like.

If you're making your own, draw small sketches of the kind of stained glass panel you want, and pencil or paint in the colors; this will help you visualize the effects of the different shapes, colors, and patterns. You can also experiment with actual glass samples, available from a stained glass supply house.

If you're having a panel custom-made, you'll probably want to work closely with the artist, relying heavily on his or her design expertise.

Stained glass windows. For a unique and original window covering, consider using a stained glass panel on a window in place of draperies or shades. To help dramatize a landscape or distant skyline, you may want to select a panel that has colors floating above clear glass. Stained glass in a clerestory window abutting an open-beam ceiling gives a room a serene feeling.

To block out an undesirable view, use a stained glass panel the size of the window; to focus attention on the view, select a rectangular or curved stained glass frame around clear glass. Clear glass mixed at random with colored glass in a single panel gives a feeling of depth.

A glass bird or foliage pattern complements house plants or enriches a garden view. If your window has many small panes, consider replacing only a pane or two for a colorful splash of light. For a room with a double-hung or horizontally

sliding window, you can create an especially rich feeling by designing each sash with different colors. The colors will change as the sashes slide over each other.

For examples of stained glass windows, see the color section, starting on page 32.

Stained glass on doors. If your local building code allows the use of stained glass, rather than tempered glass, in and around doors, think about replacing existing glass with your house number or last name designed in stained glass. French doors nicely display matching panels; a Dutch door can show off a glass panel in its top half, but retain wood below for safety.

Installation considerations

You can permanently install small stained glass panels in the same way that you install ordinary clear panes (see pages 94–95). Large panels need additional support for permanent installation; fit them into their own routed wood frames, or block their edges on both sides with wood strips nailed to the sill and window frame. Be sure to set the panel in glazing putty and caulk all outside joints.

Portable panels. If you install a panel so it can be removed easily, you can take the panel with you if you move.

To install a panel temporarily, secure it ½ to ¾ inch away from the inside of the clear pane; use wood strips between panel and sash, and brads, stops, or molding to hold the panel in place. The dead air space between the panel and the sash boosts the effective insulating value.

SKYLIGHT SHAPES

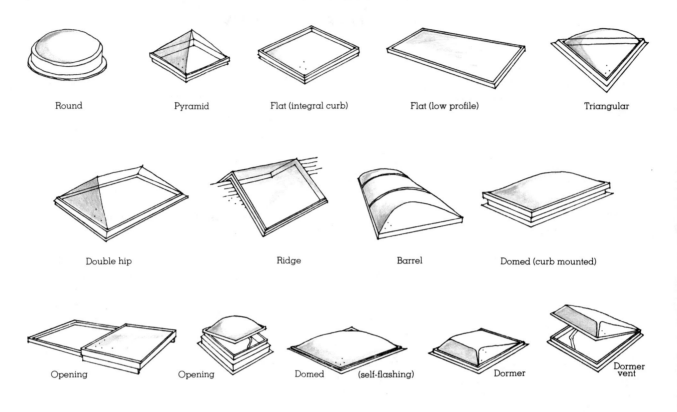

Round Pyramid Flat (integral curb) Flat (low profile) Triangular

Double hip Ridge Barrel Domed (curb mounted)

Opening Opening Domed (self-flashing) Dormer Dormer vent

. . . Continued from page 18

Some manufacturers offer motorized skylights and roof sections (actually large skylights) that can be moved to one side (see photo on page 43). If you want to open up a room to the night sky, an opening skylight may be the answer.

Basic skylight designs—both curb-mounted and self-flashing with integral curb—are available with single, double, or triple-glazed domes and with condensation gutters to prevent moisture from running down the wall.

Curb-mounted skylights are used whenever the roof is covered with heavy wood shakes, clay or concrete tiles, or slate, or whenever the roof slope is greater than 3 in 12. They are designed to be mounted on a wood curb built and flashed by the customer. The flashing keeps water from leaking in around the skylight.

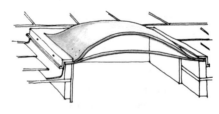

Self-flashing skylights are for use on roofs with slopes less than 3 in 12 and shingled with thin materials—wood, asphalt, or fiberglass. They are made with both an integral curb and a flange for flashing. To keep water out, a caulking compound or a sealant is applied between the flange and the roof deck, and between the flange and the roofing material.

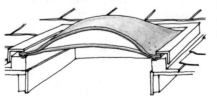

A few manufacturers offer skylights made of molded clear plastic. The plastic extends into a flange that's secured directly to the roof deck and covered with shingles.

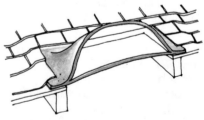

Curb and frame materials. Though some manufacturers offer a few sizes with vinyl frames, most skylights for homes have aluminum frames; the aluminum is often anodized or covered with a baked enamel finish to make it corrosion-resistant. In ocean-side environments, you may want to give further protection against the salt spray by painting the frame.

Some manufacturers use urethane, fiberglass, or even wood —all good insulators—for the curb in self-flashing skylights. Others insulate a metal frame with wood or plastic foam to provide a thermal break and prevent heat loss.

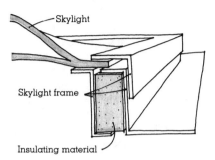

Skylight

Skylight frame

Insulating material

Skylight glazing materials. Skylights may be glazed with glass or with plastic; acrylic, polycarbonate, and fiberglass are the plastics most commonly used. Be sure to check with your building department for the types of glazing approved in your community.

Glass is used only in skylights with flat glazing surfaces. Because it's brittle, cracking and breaking if struck, glass used in skylights should be wire reinforced, tempered, or laminated. You can also use double-glazed insulating glass. Generally, glass is more expensive than plastic.

Acrylic plastic is the material that's generally used in residential skylights. Cast acrylic resists shattering and has the best weathering record of the nonglass skylight glazing materials.

Polycarbonate plastic and fiberglass have better impact resistance than acrylic, but they don't weather as well. Both materials may begin to yellow after about 5 years, eventually affecting light transmission. But some of the yellowing of polycarbonates can be removed by washing the skylight annually with approved detergents.

Some manufacturers combine acrylic with fiberglass to give the glazing the impact resistance of fiberglass and the weathering quality of acrylic.

Glazing colors for plastic have traditionally been transparent gray or bronze, translucent, and clear, but a variety of decorator colors, both transparent and semi-opaque, are also available. For information on glass glazing colors, see page 16.

Though clear plastic glazing admits the most light and heat (ideal for solar heating purposes), it may also cause glare and a spotlight effect unless oriented to the north. If it's insulated, it will show the condensation that may form between the layers.

Translucent white plastic glazing reduces the amounts of light, glare, and heat, and is manufactured in different densities. Translucent glazing diffuses light, spreading it evenly in an interior space.

Transparent bronze and gray glazings significantly lower glare and the incoming amounts of light and heat.

Ventilation. Though the majority of skylights do not open, most manufacturers offer one or two designs that can be opened to allow ventilation. You can open them either manually with the help of a pole or long cord, or automatically using a power unit that works at the touch of a button.

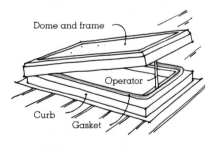

Dome and frame

Operator

Curb

Gasket

Most venting skylights open to about 45° and are equipped with insect screens. When installed on a

pitched roof with the opening side toward the downslope, these skylights can be left open when it rains. Some models have shade screens, storm panels, and power-operated exhaust fans.

If you live in a warm climate, a venting skylight may be worth the extra cost. It can effectively exhaust warm air from a room, and, combined with shading devices (see page 31) and well-placed windows, can reduce the cost of summer cooling.

Skylight energy-saving features. Skylights may be single, double, or perhaps even quadruple glazed. Though a single-glazed unit will work in temperate climates that require neither heating nor air conditioning, use a double-glazed unit at the very least in all other climates. The dead air space between the glazing layers acts as an insulator and reduces heat loss or gain to a considerable degree.

In an extremely cold climate, you can obtain extra insulation in a skylight by using a triple glazing, but at considerable expense. A more economical way is to insulate the bottom of the light shaft (see page 29).

Some manufacturers offer skylights with additional energy-saving features. Skylights with thermal breaks made of insulating material lose less heat through the frame and don't suffer from condensation on the metal surfaces. Another energy-saving feature is curbs made of insulating material in skylights with integral curbs.

Custom skylights

The world of custom skylights is almost as unlimited as the world of custom windows. Most large manufacturers will design and make a skylight that meets your special needs.

If you're covering a large area, you may have to order a custom-made skylight. It may be just about any size or shape you desire.

Home remodeling projects are not easy work. Some you can do yourself; others may require some professional help. Still others may be best left completely in the hands of professionals.

What jobs require professional help? How can you get the help you need? What is the best way to work with professionals? If you're confronted with questions like these, you'll find the following suggestions helpful as you plan and carry out your remodeling project.

When do you need professional assistance?

The effort you can contribute to any project depends on your knowledge, your abilities, your patience, and your health. If you know how to draw up plans but have a bad back, you'll need someone else to perform the physical labor. If you're able to wield a saw and hammer but can't draw a straight line, you may only need professional help to prepare working drawings.

Some people prefer to do the nonspecialized work, such as clearing the site for construction and cleaning up later, but hire experts for everything else. Others let professionals handle all the tasks from drawing plans through applying the finishing touches.

No matter whom you consult, be as precise as possible about what you want. Collect pertinent photographs from magazines, manufacturers' brochures, and advertisements. Describe the types of windows or skylights you want to use, and where you want to put them. If you have questions, write them down before the interview.

Acquiring building permits

You probably will not need a building permit for simple jobs such as replacing glass in a window or skylight or even replacing the entire unit. But for more substantial changes, like adding a window or skylight, you may need to apply for one or more permits: a structural permit and other permits for plumbing, mechanical heating or cooling, reroofing, or electrical work. Your local building department can inform you about any permits you may need.

Before you obtain permits, a building department official—a plan checker or building inspector—may need to see drawings to ensure that your remodeling concept conforms to local zoning ordinances and building codes. If the project is simple, written specifications or sketches may suffice. More complicated projects may require that the design and the working drawings be executed by an architect, designer, or state-licensed contractor.

If you plan to do all the work yourself, you may have to sign an owner-builder release exempting you from worker's compensation insurance before receiving the permits. You don't need worker's compensation insurance if a state-licensed contractor retained by you applies for the permits and does the work.

If you apply for the permits but plan to hire other people to help you with the work, you must show a Certificate of Compensation Insurance (see "Hiring workers," below).

For your permit, you'll be charged a flat rate or a percentage of the estimated cost of materials and labor. You may also need to pay a plan-checking fee.

If you're acting as your own contractor, you must ask the building department to inspect the work as it progresses. Adding a window usually requires only two inspections: one after the framing is completed, and another one after the job is finished. More complicated jobs require more inspections.

Failure to obtain a permit or an inspection may result in your having to dismantle completed work.

Architect or designer—which one do you need?

Either an architect or a designer can draw up plans acceptable to building department officials; each can also specify materials for a contractor to order. They can send out bids, help you select a contractor, and supervise the contractor's performance to ensure that your plans and time schedule are being followed. Some architects and designers even double as their own contractors.

Most states do not require designers to be licensed, as architects must; many designers charge less for their labor. If stress calculations must be made, designers need state-licensed engineers to design the structure and sign the working drawings; architects can do their own calculations.

Many architects are members of American Institute of Architects (AIA), and many designers belong to the American Institute of Building Designers (AIBD). Each association has a code of ethics and a continuing program to inform members about the latest building materials and techniques.

Usually, architects and designers don't charge for time spent in an exploratory interview. For plans, you'll probably be charged on an hourly basis. If you want an architect or designer to select the contractor and keep an eye on construction, plan to pay either an hourly rate or a percentage of the cost of materials and labor—10 to 15 percent is typical.

If your project is very small, you may be able to entice an apprentice or drafter working in an architect or designer's office to draw plans for you. Plan to pay by the hour.

Choosing a contractor

Contractors do more than construction. Often, they're skilled drafters, able to draw plans acceptable to building department officials; they can also obtain the necessary building permits. A contractor's experience and technical know-how may even end up saving you money.

If you decide to use a contractor, ask architects, designers, and friends for recommendations. To compare bids for the actual construction, contact at least three state-licensed contractors and give each one either an exact description and sketches of the desired remodeling or plans and specifications prepared by an architect or designer. Include a detailed account of who will be responsible for what work.

Most contractors will bid a fixed price for a remodeling job, to be paid in installments based on the amount of work completed. Many states limit the amount of "good faith" money

that contractors can request before work begins.

Though some contractors may want a fee based on a percentage of the cost of materials and labor, it's usually wiser to insist on a fixed-price bid. This protects you both against an unexpected rise in the cost of materials (assuming the contractor does the buying) and against the chance that the work will take more time, adding to your labor costs.

But don't be tempted to make price your only criterion for selection; reliability, quality of work, and on-time performance are also important. Ask each contractor for the names and phone numbers of their customers. Call several and ask them how they feel about the contractor; if you can, inspect the contractor's work.

Make sure your agreement with the contractor you've selected includes the following items in writing: plans and material specifications, services to be supplied, cost, method and schedule of payment, time schedule, and warranty against defects. Not only is the contract binding to both parties, but also it minimizes problems by defining responsibilities. Changing your mind once construction starts usually requires a contract modification, involving both additional expense and delays.

Hiring workers

Even when you're operating as your own contractor, you may want to hire workers on an hourly basis for their specialized skills or their brawn.

If you hire such help, you may have to provide worker's compensation insurance to cover possible job-

related injuries. Though provisions vary from state to state, compensation insurance usually reimburses the worker for wages lost and for the cost of medical treatment. Worker's compensation policies are available from insurance brokers, insurance companies, and sometimes from state funds.

As an employer, you must withhold and remit state and federal income taxes; withhold, remit, and contribute to Social Security; and pay state unemployment insurance. For information, talk to a building department official, or look under the subheading "Taxes" under your state in the white pages of your telephone directory.

Where to look for assistance

The best way to find competent architects, designers, contractors, and workers is to ask friends and neighbors who used professionals in a project similar to yours. You can also seek referrals from retail building materials outlets (listed in the Yellow Pages under "Hardware" and "Lumber").

The Yellow Pages list design professionals under "Architects," "Building Designers," or "Drafting Services"; look for contractors to handle a remodeling project under "Contractors—Alteration" and contractors for major projects under "Contractors—Building, General."

For more specialized assistance, look under one or more of the following headings: "Carpenters," "Electric Contractors," "Glass—Auto, Plate, Window," "Plumbing Contractors," "Roofing Contractors," "Skylights," or "Windows."

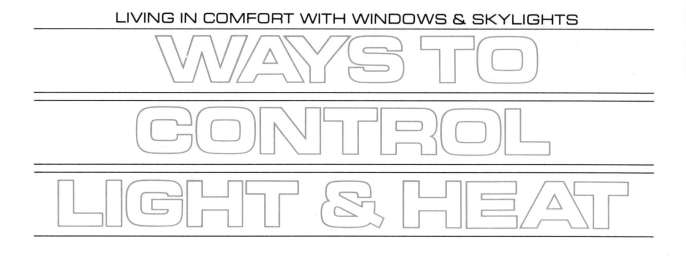

WAYS TO CONTROL LIGHT & HEAT

oorly insulated or incorrectly oriented windows and skylights are a costly liability, for they allow an unwanted exchange of heat between the inside and outside of your home. Fifteen to 35 percent of your home's total heat loss comes from windows and skylights.

Fortunately, you can prevent this expensive energy loss in a number of ways. One effective method of reducing heat loss is insulating your openings, either with extra layers of glazing or with movable insulating systems (insulated window coverings). You may also want to consider the use of shutters, blinds, drapery liners, and shades. Technological research prompted by continually soaring energy costs promises even better products in the future.

All these methods of thermal control are discussed on the following pages. In addition to reducing your fuel bills, installing devices that improve the thermal performance of windows and skylights may help you qualify for tax credits from federal and state governments. Check with the federal and state tax agencies for approved devices and amount of tax credit.

HOW HEAT IS LOST OR GAINED

Heat flows in one direction—from warmer areas to cooler ones. If the air outside your house is cooler than the air inside, your inside heat will seek any possible route by which to continue its flow to the cold air outside. Conversely, hot air from outside will flow into the house's cooler interior when it's hotter outside than inside.

Though windows generally make up less of your home's total surface area than walls or roof, they lose or gain much more heat per square foot, especially if they're single glazed, because they're less resistant to heat flow. Heat transfer can occur through the glazing, through the muntins and sash frames, and through the fixed frame. If the window or skylight is poorly fitted or sealed, heat can escape or enter through cracks and gaps.

How does heat move?

Heat has three ways of moving from one spot to another: conduction, convection, and radiation. Because they apply to all heat loss or gain, these three concepts are fundamen-

tal to an understanding of heat conservation. The illustration below shows how heat moves.

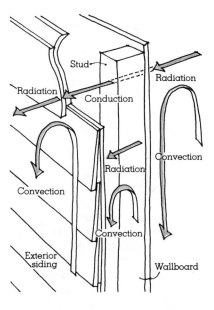

Conduction occurs when heat, passing from molecule to molecule, moves *through* a solid, liquid, or gas to an adjoining solid, liquid, or gas. Materials like aluminum, steel, and glass conduct heat more readily than plastic and wood.

To minimize conduction losses in windows and skylights, materials that are good thermal conductors must be used for window construction or must separate the inside and outside surfaces of the window or skylight.

Convection is the movement of air that carries heat from warmer surfaces to cooler ones. As air warms, it expands, becomes lighter, and rises. Then, as it gives off heat to surrounding objects, it cools, contracts, becomes denser, and sinks.

When warm room air hits cold window glass, the air is cooled and sinks to the floor, allowing more warm air to contact the glass. This creates a convective current of rising warm air and falling cool air. By placing an insulation barrier between the warm air and the cold glass, you can slow or stop this current.

Infiltration —energy loss caused by cold or warm air leaking to the inside or outside—is another form of convection and can be a major source of energy drain in a house. A poorly fitted, single-glazed window may lose twice as much heat through gaps and cracks in the frame as through the entire glass area. These losses, though, can be reduced by caulking and weatherstripping (see page 93; also see the *Sunset* book *Do-It-Yourself Insulation & Weatherstripping*).

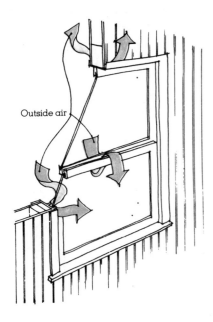

Outside air

Radiation is the transmission of heat through space by wave motion. All warm objects emit radiant energy. When this energy strikes a cool surface, the cool object absorbs some energy as heat and reflects the remainder. We receive the sun's energy through radiation; we also receive warmth from a hot stove across the room through radiation.

But the sun's radiant energy is different from the radiant energy emitted by warm objects in a room. The sun emits short-wave or near-infrared radiation that passes through window and skylight glazing; the radiant energy from objects in a room is long-wave or far-infrared. Too weak to pass directly through the glazing, this room-generated radiation is absorbed by it, and in the case of single glazing, is reradiated to the cooler outdoor air.

To reduce winter radiation losses, a thermal barrier impervious to the long-wave room temperature radiation must be placed on the inside or outside of the glass. To eliminate summer radiation gains, you'll need a barrier that keeps the sun's short-wave and long-wave radiation from penetrating the room.

REDUCING HEAT LOSS

Even with a careful orientation, your windows or skylights will still lose a considerable amount of heat to the cold outdoors in winter. The worst losses occur at night, after the sun stops warming your home through south-facing windows. You can reduce this heat loss either by adding a layer of glazing to your windows and skylights, or by covering the glass with an insulating material, or by doing both.

Glazing systems: single, double, or more

Adding one or two layers of glazing—glass or plastic—improves the thermal resistance (R value) of your window by creating a dead air space between the glazing layers. Since air is a poor conductor of heat, the strong convective currents that can hasten heat exchange are prevented from forming, as long as the air space between the glazings doesn't exceed 3 inches.

You can obtain an extra layer of glazing either by putting in double or triple-glazed window units or by installing storm windows.

One annoying problem with multiple glazings is the possibility of condensation between the panes. But most prefabricated insulated (double or triple-glazed) units are made with the two panes of glass hermetically sealed at the edges (which prevents moisture from penetrating at all) or with the panes separated by metal spacers filled with a drying agent to absorb moisture and bonded to the edges of the glass with a sealant.

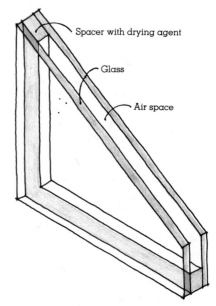

Spacer with drying agent

Glass

Air space

Condensation can occur with storm windows if they don't fit tightly, or if they're installed over a leaky window. Weatherstripping a poorly fitted window usually solves the problem (see page 93; also see the *Sunset* book *Do-It-Yourself Insulation & Weatherstripping*).

Single glazing vs. double glazing. Strictly speaking, a single-glazed window with a covering that achieves R-5 insulation (see next page) and a seal around the edges performs better than an uninsulated, double-glazed window. But a single layer of glass becomes very cold at night. Unless the covering has a tight edge seal, warm room air, carried upward by convection across the glass surface, is cooled and forced to give up its moisture, causing condensation. To be fully effective, the insulating covering must be put in place every night. A double-glazed window without an edge-sealed insulating covering may also collect condensation, but usually to a lesser degree.

Double glazing vs. triple glazing. Compared with single glazing, a double-glazed window cuts heat loss by 45 percent; a triple-glazed window cuts the loss by an additional 10 to 15 percent. But keep in mind that the third layer of glazing also reduces light transmission and the amount of solar radiation entering the house by about 10 percent compared with double glazing—an important consideration for south-facing windows. For north, east, or west-facing windows which contribute little or no solar heat in winter, triple glazing is cost effective only in very cold climates.

Storm windows. Traditionally, storm windows were a single pane of glass set in a wood or aluminum frame, installed seasonally on the outside of a window. Today, though, you can buy storm windows that are removable or permanent; glazed with glass or plastic; set in wood, aluminum, or plastic frames; installed on the outside or inside of a window. Some permanent units are designed on a double or triple-track system with glass and insect-screening panels for year-round use (see above right).

If you're planning to buy storm windows, keep the following considerations in mind:

• Storm windows with wood or plastic sashes may be your best buy, since these materials are poor heat conductors.

• Combination triple-track

storm windows may not seal well, allowing air to infiltrate around the window components.

• Plastic units are usually cheaper than glass, and, depending on the type of plastic used, may last for up to 15 years.

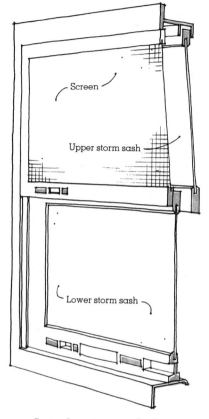

Interior storm windows can be made of flexible or rigid plastic, or glass. They can be used with existing single or double-glazed windows for additional insulation.

Some interior storm windows have a removable lower glass panel that can be replaced with a screen for summer use. A vinyl gasket holds the panels in an aluminum frame; spring-loaded clips secure the unit against an existing window frame. Vinyl weatherstripping helps to ensure a tight seal against the casing.

Flexible plastic units are made from either polyvinyl chloride, polyester, or mylar film stretched over an aluminum frame or polyester film stretched across a plastic frame. A recent innovation is a flexible film made of high-strength polyester laminated over weather-resistant acryl-

ic. Strong enough for indoor or outdoor use, this film comes in a kit.

You can also apply an inexpensive polyethylene film to the inside of your windows. But it will have to be replaced within a year or two because of yellowing, distortion, or tearing. Rigid plastic sheets of acrylic or polystyrene can be attached to existing windows with adhesive or magnetic strips; or they can be set in a vinyl frame that attaches in the same way.

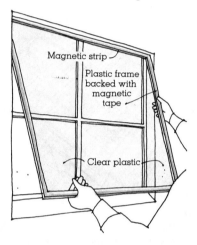

Innovative glazing. Simply by adding a pane, you can convert your single-glazed window to a double-glazed one at half the cost of purchasing a new insulated unit. A trained installer adds a metal spacer filled with drying agent, the pane, and a sealant, which is then cured with an electric heating wire to provide a permanent seal.

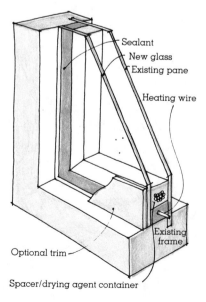

Also available for window application are rigid plastic sheets molded from acrylic or polycarbonate with internal ribs that create pockets of dead air; since the ribs limit visibility, you won't want to use these sheets if a clear view is important.

Insulating glass that incorporates a radiation-reflective film, or "heat mirror," is now on the market. Polyester plastic film is coated on one side with a layer of metal only atoms thick. Though transparent to light, it reflects long-wave, room-temperature radiation. In effect, it's transparent insulation.

HEAT-INSULATING GLASS

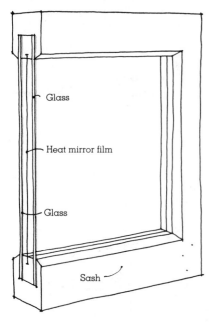

Glass

Heat mirror film

Glass

Sash

Movable insulation

Shutters, shades, and other insulating devices that can be either left in place or removed to expose the glazing come in a variety of forms and materials. You can install these movable devices outside the window (best for keeping the heat out), between two layers of glazing, or on the inside of a window (best for keeping the heat in).

As you compare the various devices to find the one that best suits your needs and budget, keep the following criteria in mind.

Thermal resistance or R value. This is the resistance of a material to the passage of heat. Double the R value and you'll reduce the heat loss by 50 percent. Studies show that a thermal resistance of R-5 offers optimal reduction in heat loss through a window or skylight. Increasing R values beyond this point may not always be cost effective, especially when the insulating device is used mainly at night. In any case, features such as a tight seal and ease of operation also affect the amount of heat loss. Another point to remember is that manufacturers may give you the combined R value of a bare window with *their* insulating device (counting the insulating value of the dead air space between the glazing and their insulation).

Edge seals. To prevent the warm room air from infiltrating and setting up a convection current between the glazing and insulation, the insulating device must form a tight seal against the window (see below). A loose seal not only promotes convective losses, but also causes mildew-forming and sill-rotting condensation. Even an R-3 insulating device that seals tightly against the window can perform better than an R-8 device that does not.

TYPICAL EDGE SEAL

Window shade

Hinge

Wood strip

Window trim

Stool

Moisture protection. Insulating devices lined (on the side facing the room) with a vapor barrier—a material impervious to moisture—help prevent condensation. This is especially important in cold climates.

Durability. The hardware of any insulating device that's removed and replaced daily eventually wears out; check to see that the hardware is sturdy and can be easily replaced.

Safety. Many devices use plastic foam, film, or synthetic fibers that are fire or smoke hazards if not properly covered. Aluminum foil-facing or a coating of fire-retardant paint reduces this hazard. Also, heavy shutters that hinge at the top can be hazardous if they're located where people can walk into them.

Ease of operation. Even an R-10 shutter won't reduce your heating bills if it's so cumbersome to operate that you rarely use it. To be effective, any insulating device must be used regularly and punctually. The easier it is to operate, the more likely you are to use it.

Esthetics. Make the device as attractive as you can; if it enhances your interior decor, you'll use it regularly.

Exterior devices. Though they may be esthetically appealing, exterior shutters are more expensive than interior shutters or shades that provide equal or better protection. In addition, any insulation installed on the outside of a window must be strong enough to withstand the effects of wind, rain, snow, and sun.

Rolling shutters are made from interlocking wood, hollow plastic, or polyurethane-filled aluminum slats that slide in rigid tracks. Operated from the inside by either a hand crank or a motor, the shutters have slats that can be tightly closed or left open a little to admit some air and light. One of these is illustrated below.

Though they provide only a moderate reduction in heat loss, these shutters can be used the year around; they also provide privacy and security.

Hinged shutters made from foam faced with wood or aluminum are available from some manufacturers. Each side of the wood-faced shutter is made of two panels that slide and fold out of the way when cranked from the inside. The aluminum-faced shutter, also crank operated, is top hinged; it can be used as an awning in summer.

Between-the-glass insulation. A very effective device uses polystyrene beads to insulate the 3-inch space between two sealed layers of glazing. At the touch of a button, a pump fills or empties the space in minutes. The beads are stored in concealed wall storage tanks when

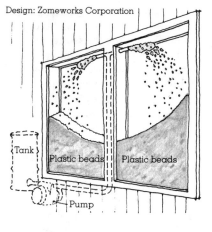

Design: Zomeworks Corporation

not in use. In summer, the bead-filled wall insulates against the heat of the sun.

Interior devices. Windows can be insulated from the inside with thermally lined draperies, pop-in shutters, or rolling shutters or shades.

Draperies lined with heat-reflective aluminized polyester or bubble polyethylene sandwiched between two layers of fabric can reduce heat loss. With either method, the lining can be hung separately behind the draperies, its edges sealed to the window. The aluminized lining is also available as a rolling shade.

Liners made of a reflective material are useful for both winter and summer heat control. In winter, the reflective side of the liner should face into the room; for summer comfort, hang the reflective side facing out.

Conventional draperies made of nonporous material provide some protection from losses through radiation, but to be noticeably effective against convective losses their edges must be sealed.

Enclosing the top of the drapery in a valance, weighing down the hem, and sealing the side edges to the window frame help keep in heat (see next page).

WINDOW INSULATION & SHADE

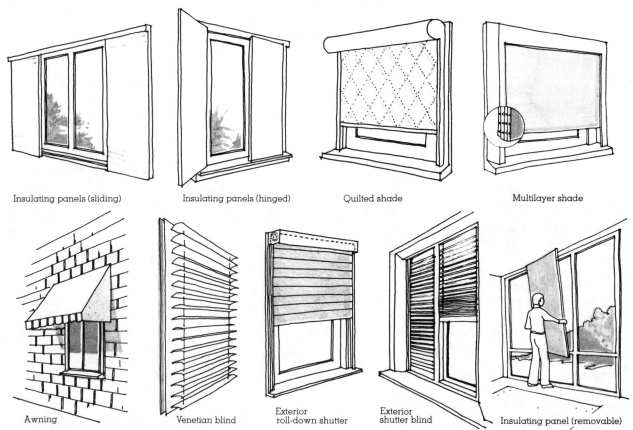

Insulating panels (sliding)

Insulating panels (hinged)

Quilted shade

Multilayer shade

Awning

Venetian blind

Exterior roll-down shutter

Exterior shutter blind

Insulating panel (removable)

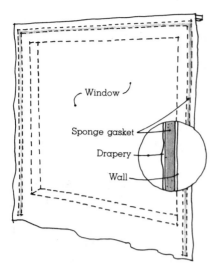

Removable insulating panels are inexpensive and effective interior insulation. You can make pop-ins from rigid foam boards cut to fit the window glazing or sash. Either fit the panels into the opening using friction, or attach them to the glass or sash with continuous magnetic strips. Some manufacturers offer foam faced with aluminum foil to take advantage of the metal's heat-reflection and fire-retardant qualities. The foil face can be painted or decorated.

Pop-in shutters sitting directly against the glass permit practically no air movement behind them; but the metal strips around the perimeter of the glass may be objectionable for year-round use. The effectiveness of other pop-in shutters depends on the tightness of their edge seals.

Another type of interior shutter is made of a foam core sandwiched between wood panels with flexible foam or neoprene strips on the frame to ensure a tight seal. Hinged at the sides, the shutters usually rest against the wall when they're open.

Also available is a urethane panel encased in plastic; stored inside a wall, the panel slides out to cover the window when desired.

Interior shades can be made from quilted fabric, layers of plastic or nylon, or hollow rigid plastic slats.

Quilted shades can have as many as five layers of fabric—a core layer of reflective vapor barrier fabric sandwiched between polyester fiberfill and outer fabric coverings. The bottom of the shade is weighted; to reduce air infiltration, the sides slide in a track attached to the window frame.

The layers in the plastic or nylon shades expand to form dead air pockets when the shades are pulled down. The sides of the shades are enclosed in tracks to prevent air infiltraton. One type offers three plastic roll-up shades mounted in the same frame: the transparent shade provides solar heat, the reflective one insulates in winter, and the third one controls summer sun.

Like roll-down exterior shutters, shades made of plastic slats slide in side tracks and can be operated either manually or automatically. Each hollow slat forms an insulating air pocket.

Shutters for skylights. In addition to the louvered shutters illustrated on page 31, you can install sliding insulated panels that pull across the skylight to prevent heat loss at night and in cold weather.

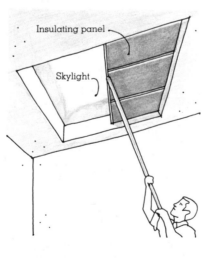

Another shutter has aluminum louvers filled with fiberglass insulation; the louvers open during the day and close at night by the movement of heat-sensitive freon between reservoirs attached to opposite ends of the shutter. When closed, this shutter achieves a tighter seal than the wood shutter described above. For convenience, a manual override allows you to control the louver operation.

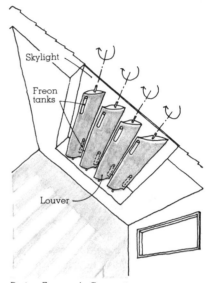

Design: Zomeworks Corporation

SHADING FOR SUMMER COMFORT

Though desirable in winter, the sun's heat can turn your house into a solar oven in summer.

Shading devices can prevent this unwanted heat from penetrating the interior of your home. Your choice of devices depends on your climate, latitude, existing vegetation, prevailing winds, view, and house orientation and style.

Roof overhangs and awnings

Any shading device—an overhang, an awning, or even trees and vines—that keeps the sun off your window altogether works best to keep down indoor temperatures.

An overhang, though, usually has to be planned as part of the original construction, and its projection size carefully calculated to exclude the high summer sun, yet admit the low winter sun for effective solar heating. Most effective on south-facing windows, overhangs give little protection against the low-angle sun on the east and west sides of a house.

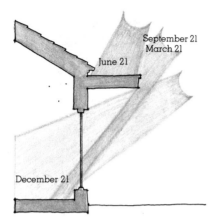

Awnings are just as effective as overhangs on south-facing windows; movable types that can be angled, depending on the sun's position, extend the hours of protection. Fabric awnings usually have to be replaced after about 6 years; metal awnings are noisy during heavy rains.

It's best to install both awnings and overhangs with a gap between the wall and the unit for venting the warm air.

Exterior shutters, blinds, and screens

Another solution for reducing summer heat gain is to install a screening device immediately outside your window. Most exterior shutters, blinds, and screens block the sun, either partially or completely, depending on their design and method of operation. But they also limit the amount of light and air and restrict your view.

Shutters. Some shutters used for reducing winter heat loss (see page 28) can also be used for summer sun control.

Other shutters for summer use include those with horizontal louvers, which work best for south-facing windows, and those with vertical louvers for windows on the east and west sides.

Shutters made from wood or aluminum slats fixed at an angle to block direct sunlight are also available. Some companies even make windows incorporating adjustable external louvered shading devices.

Blinds. Several manufacturers offer exterior blinds made from wood or aluminum slats; they can be operated either manually or automatically. The slats can be tilted to allow some light, view, and ventilation, or they can be closed.

Screens. Another way to block the sun on the outside is by putting up louvered or woven screens. Louvered sun screens consist of an array of tiny aluminum louvers set at a fixed angle to block direct sunlight. Most woven sun screens are made from fiberglass yarns. Available in different colors and densities, they cut heat gain anywhere from 45 to 80 percent.

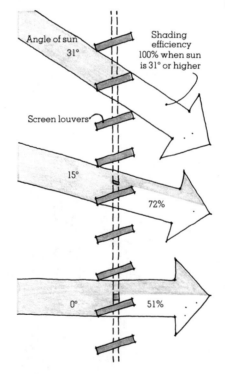

You can buy screens for standard-size windows already framed in aluminum mounts; or buy screening material and hardware to make your own. You can also have screens custom-made to fit your window.

Screens allow some view and ventilation, but may reduce the amount of light entering a room by up to 80 percent. When mounted on the outside, all except the movable variety prevent the operation of outward-opening windows.

Sun-control glass and film

Sun-control glass may be reflective or heat absorbing. Reflecting glass—glass with a thin, reflective coating bonded to it—provides better sun control, reducing heat gain up to 80 percent. But it also reduces light transmission by as much as 70 percent. One manufacturer of reflective glass offers panels that can be fitted into existing window screen slots.

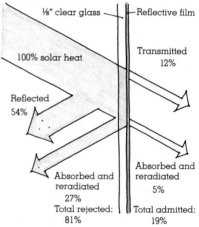

Films for solar control are made from self-sticking plastic and are applied to the inside surface of window glass. The films may be reflective or tinted (heat-absorbing). As with coatings, the reflective types perform better than the tinted ones. Films are available in different colors and light transmission values; the denser the film, the less light it admits.

Films are a relatively inexpensive sun-control solution, but since most cannot be removed seasonally, they have limited use in any but warm climates. Though most also scratch easily and require careful handling and cleaning, a hardier film that can be easily removed in winter is now available.

Interior blinds, shades, and drapes

Conventional horizontal louvers (venetian blinds), as well as the newer vertical blinds, can reduce heat gain by at least 20 percent and up to 70 percent. Vertical blinds work best on the east and west sides of a house. You can choose from a wide selection of materials, including aluminum, fabric, plastic, and wood (either plain or covered with wallpaper or fabric). Horizontal blinds can be raised and vertical blinds drawn to one side; both types can be manually or motor operated. The blind slats can be adjusted, too.

When completely closed, blinds keep the heat trapped between them and the window, but they also block the view and a good part of the daylight. You can overcome these disadvantages with a new product made from aluminized polyester; this pleated blind provides some control of heat gain and allows an outside view. Also available are blinds, louvers, and curtains of varying densities for different degrees of sun control.

Conventional vinyl-coated interior shades let in some daylight, but block the view. Semitransparent shades made of tinted, reflective, patterned, or perforated materials offer a wide selection of light and heat-transmission values. One type of interior shade that rolls up from the bottom can control sunlight without obstructing the view.

Unless they're lined with a reflective material (see page 28), conventional draperies and curtains offer the least resistance to solar gain. But they provide more ventilation, view, and light control than do most other shading devices.

You can also use accordion-style draperies of embossed, textured aluminum; they slide in horizontal channels at both top and bottom. Available in many different colors, these draperies allow some daylight to penetrate even when they're closed, and perform better than standard or reflective-lined draperies.

Between-the-glass devices

Several manufacturers supply double-glazed insulating panels with louvered blinds between the two panes. Using a control on the window frame, you can adjust the angle of the louvers from the inside.

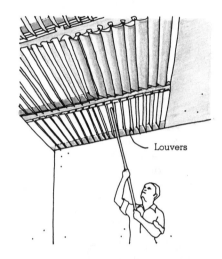

Sun control for skylights

Skylight manufacturers, as well as companies that make shutters, shades, and blinds for windows, offer several standard or custom-made shading devices for skylights. Among the items you can purchase are external awnings, interior shades, and blinds. One sophisticated skylight comes with a motorized pleated shade that stacks to one side when not in use.

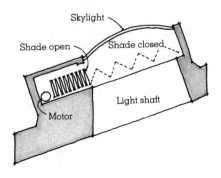

Skylight
Shade open — Shade closed
Light shaft
Motor

Though blinds and shades for skylights usually are designed for inside installation, you may be able to install an additional dome of translucent, reflective, or heat-absorbing material on the outside.

A jalousie-style window with wood, rather than glass, louvers can be installed beneath a skylight, and is an effective sun-control device. Painted white on one side, the louvers reflect solar radiation up to 90 percent when they're closed.

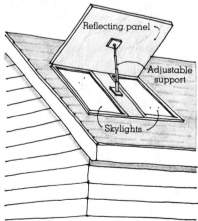

Louvers

Another way to catch or deflect the sun is by mounting a movable reflector on the roof over the skylight. In summer, you lower the reflector to shade the skylight; this reduces solar gain by 80 percent. In winter, you raise the reflector to intercept the low-angle winter sun.

Design: Jonathan Hammond, Living Systems

Reflecting panel
Adjustable support
Skylights

IDEAS FOR WINDOWS & SKYLIGHTS

Probably no other single feature of a room's design contributes more to its character than its openings, whether they're windows, skylights, or a combination of both. Correct selection and placement of these openings can make the difference between an airy room magically alive with natural light, and one plagued by glare and heat—or even gloom and cold.

Consider the functions of windows. They're more than just holes in the fabric of your house. A well-designed window can open interior space to the outdoors; it can bring in welcome—and needed—light. You can even design windows that will help reduce your utility bills.

Some windows are show-stoppers. Dramatic size, shape, and division of a single area into small panes are just a few of the ways a window takes on character. Colorful stained glass, finely beveled glass, even glass blocks add a splash of color, a touch of nostalgia.

Skylights bring their own special drama to a room. Frequently used in contemporary design, they are equally at home in traditional houses. Skylights range from simple domes you can buy at home improvement centers to major design elements dominating a remodel or new home. At both ends of the spectrum, their potential for adding and balancing light is great.

This chapter is designed to set your feet on the path to successful use of windows and skylights in both new construction and remodeling. On these pages we feature outstanding designs ranging in style from traditional to contemporary, from budget-conscious to sky's-the-limit. All have a common thread: each is a successful solution to a problem, a problem faced—and resolved—by someone like you.

Our gallery is divided into sections on attention-getting windows (beginning on page 34), skylights (page 38), daylighting (page 44), and maximizing the view (page 48). Additional sections deal with special problems—and opportunities —such as entry lighting (beginning on page 52), window nooks (page 54), use of specialty glass (page 56), and sun shading (page 64). A section on greenhouse windows begins on page 58, followed by ideas for passive solar applications, starting on page 62.

If you've been hovering on the brink of building your dream home or you're just anxious to do something about the sunless bathroom where the towels never dry, or the minuscule window punched in the wall facing the best view, read on: this chapter may just nudge you over the edge and into action.

Almost Alfresco
Dramatic window-wall and acrylic bubble skylight bring light and view to remodeled kitchen and breakfast area. Windows' double glazing helps conserve heat. Architect: John Galbraith.

ATTENTION-GETTERS

ARCHES, CIRCLES, DIVIDERS & DIAMONDS—SHAPELY WINDOWS PROVE YOU NEEDN'T THINK SQUARE

Bubble Bath
Playful circular window adds sprightly note to master bathroom; cheerful tile maintains tone. Window brings in light, looks out onto private deck. Architects: Fisher-Friedman.

Picture Perfect
Graceful arch breaks up rectangular opening and frames view from attractive dining room. Layers of bender board covered with wallboard form arch. Aluminum-framed, double-glazed windows were made to measure, then simply nailed in place, flashed, and caulked. Architects: Jacobson/ Silverstein/Winslow.

Glass Gable
Through sensitive glazing, remodeled attic window lets in additional daylight, preserves privacy at night. Windows make good use of space, yet permit structural support between panes. Upside-down roller shades rise just past halfway and are held in place with small brass clips. Architect: Weldon Jean Skirvin.

Pure Delight
Taking good advantage of gable space, windows in remodeled bedroom become dramatic focal point. Fixed glass arcs toward light; small-paned casements admit fresh air. Above bed, interior window lets light into dressing area. Tinted, transparent shade hidden behind beam tames heat of late-afternoon sun. Architect: William B. Remick.

Virtuoso Performance
More than fine craftsmanship is apparent in these beautiful windows. Breaking up large expanse of glass livens room without affecting light, air, and view brought in by windows. Architects: Eden & Eden.

Turning Corners
Skillful use of silicone-sealed, butted-glass corners enhances lofty den. In clerestory, butted corner makes ceiling appear weightless; in large window, corner suggests more space than it actually encloses—a useful illusion for small room. Though structurally unnecessary, bold horizontal muntins lend human scale to large, light-gathering window. Design: MLA/Architects.

By the Bay

Bay window behind cooktop allows chef to concoct culinary delights while enjoying garden and keeping an eye on little ones. Small panes add country charm. Architect: William B. Remick.

Top o' the Morning

Opening up to rafters and adding windows gives breakfast area much-needed light and air. Arched windows are sized to width of fixed panes below. Casements on both sides of fixed panes open for ventilation. Architect: William B. Remick.

Second Time Around

Breakfast area in remodeled Craftsman-era house features new French doors and casements with finely detailed leaded panes. Windows replace double-hung units. Inserts of tinted glass enliven design. Architect: Mark Tarasuck. Window design: Vance Southwick.

SKYLIGHTS PLAIN & FANCY

FROM BASIC BUBBLE TO RADICAL REMODEL—LETTING THE DAY LIGHT YOUR HOME

Air for the Attic
European rotary window tilts for breath of fresh air and for easy cleaning. Movable mini-blinds control sunlight. Widely available in this country, unit incorporates rainproof vent to permit ventilation on wet days. Architect: William Zimmerman.

In the Bedroom
Tucked into ceiling, east-facing skylight in remodeled bedroom captures sun's early rays. Small-paned Dutch door brings in additional morning light. Architect: William B. Remick.

In the Kitchen
Pair of wire-reinforced glass skylights, mounted on low curbs, adds finishing touch to open-beam kitchen ceiling. Architect: Ted T. Tanaka.

Brightening a Bathroom
Long, narrow insulated skylight provides abundant natural light for bathroom; incandescent bulbs mounted in shaft provide light by night. Angled wallboard shaft connects ceiling and roof openings, helps diffuse light. Architect: Jennifer Clements.

In the Attic, Over the Stairs
Large "double bubble" skylight acts as window for attic remodel and as skylight, via fenced-in glass panel in floor, for stairwell below. Architect: Jennifer Clements.

For the Artist
Glazed roof is ideal light source for ceramics studio. Tempered glass assures safety; floor, tile over concrete, stores solar heat, helps warm room. Architect: Ron Senna.

For the Collector
Unbreakable polycarbonate ridge skylight lies along roof plane. Light box below directs and diffuses light to protect art collection. Artificial lights in box provide nighttime illumination. Architect: Peter C. Rodi/Designbank.

For the Cook

Shed skylight marks transition between dining area add-on, left, and remodeled kitchen, right. Replacing windows in wall that once existed where upper edge of skylight now meets the house, large skylight keeps kitchen bright. Architect: William B. Remick.

For the Diners

Reinforced plastic panels diffuse light from large dome skylight above dining area. Set in exact center of house, skylight brightens interior without fading fabrics and is thermally efficient. Mirror in far wall expands space, improves light distribution. Architect: Fred Briggs.

Light for Every Room

Ambitious remodel features dramatic, whole-house skylight. Ceiling was opened up and rafters of hip roof exposed; new post-and-beam structure replaces bearing walls. Perching above it all, copper-flashed glass skylight casts light throughout house (see photo at left). Plant mezzanine running length of skylight marks old ceiling height. Design: MLA/Architects.

Sharing the Light

View from bedroom, at opposite end of house pictured at right, shows how wall and ceiling cut-outs allow light to fall into areas not directly under skylight. Design: MLA/Architects.

Under the Big Top

Two large acrylic domes mark apex of tentlike cabin roof and light entire interior. Occupants of loft enjoy vista of forest by day, moon and stars by night. Loft's railing increases amount of light that can penetrate to living room below. Architect: Obie Bowman.

Open to the Sky

Open, motorized glass roof lets soft breezes in; closed, it retains heat stored in dark masonry floor. Either way, skylight illuminates wide expanse of interior space. Architect: Don Knorr.

Universal Light

Forming both roof and ceiling of remodeled home, glass-fiber-reinforced polyester panels admit soft, diffuse light to most rooms. Panels consist of two layers of plastic separated and supported by aluminum core frame. Result is a light, stiff structural material with good insulating properties. House sits on narrow lot, with sidewalks and neighbors close at hand; panels brighten interior with no loss of privacy. Design: MLA/Architects.

BRINGING IN LIGHT

LIGHT SHAFTS, CLERESTORIES, GLAZED ROOFS & GABLES CAPTURE LIGHT FROM ALOFT

Sky High
Multistory light shaft brings sun into all levels of tall house; shown is dining room on lowest level. Double-glazed windows facing south are designed for solar gain; mini-blinds control amount. Shaft allows air circulation between levels. Architect: The Hastings Group.

Planned for Privacy
Large window in stairwell lights areas on two floors, brightens pathway up and down. Stained glass not only adds strong decorative element, but also hides view of busy highway just outside. Architect: Morris Skendarian.
Glass design: Jos Maes.

A Subtle Touch
Kitchen remodel creates open ceiling for light, airy feeling. Arched window enhances desired effect at minimum expense. (Try to imagine room without it.) Architect: William B. Remick.

Cool Brilliance
Solarium roof in warm climate is designed for maximum light, minimum heat. Roof's saw-toothed profile features glass panels on north, opaque panels on south. Opaque panels can be fitted with active solar collectors for domestic hot-water system. Landscape architect: Woody Dike.

Kitchen Cul-de-Sac
Small clerestory windows brighten and
warm windowless kitchen corner.
Loss of cabinet space was small price to
pay. Architect: William B. Remick.

Solar Dining Room
South-facing clerestories admit warmth
of low, winter sun; overhang above
blocks sun in summer. Relationship
between size of window and depth of
overhang was carefully thought out
for region with cool winters, hot
summers. Architects: Jacobson/
Silverstein/Winslow.

Abracadabra!

A touch of architectural sleight-of-hand floats bedroom ceiling above narrow clerestories. (Divisions between panes conceal supports.) Butted-glass corner under cantilevered roof adds insult to injury inflicted on law of gravity. Design: MLA/Architects.

Balancing Act

Combination of gable window and side-wall clerestories balances light in remodeled living room. Light passing through room brightens roofed patio just outside French doors. New raised ceiling made clerestories possible—and necessary for illumination. Design: MLA/Architects.

All the Answers

Clerestory opens to provide light and air, preserve privacy in master bedroom. Proximity of neighbors dictated use of high window, but building to setback line precluded roof overhang for shade. Solution: clerestory was notched back into room. Architect: Bert Tarayao.

MAXIMIZING THE VIEW

DESIGNING WINDOWS TO GET THE MOST FROM WELL-FAVORED SITES

Window Wall
Even on rainy days, two-story glass wall seemingly disappears into landscape beyond. Double-glazed windows are made from sliding-door replacement glass for substantial cost-savings. Strategically placed skylight keeps fireplace from appearing too dark against bright wall. Design: William Young.

Up, Down & All Around
Though cozy fires occasionally force residents to turn their backs on the view, waterside home remodel offers every opportunity for outlooks. Shed-roof addition features large skylight, high and low windows. Architects: Hewitt/Daly.

Wraparound

Large plate-glass windows turn corner with no interruption, thanks to use of butted glass. Corner roof supports would have divided lovely harbor scene into two "pictures"—one on each wall. Design: MLA/Architects.

Detour

Jog in bedroom wall creates comfortable spot to observe pool activities and city beyond. Windows in attractive seating nook allow owners to feel surrounded by view, yet sheltered. Modern casements admit plenty of fresh air, allow access to both surfaces from inside or outside house. Design: MLA/Architects.

Living in the View

Coastal view envelops those who enjoy deep window seat. Tinted glass roof reduces heat build-up; screened awning windows below admit fresh air. Architect: Fred Briggs.

Bathroom Extension

Bathers in tub tucked under eaves gaze
out onto private deck. Part of remodeled
master-bedroom suite, bath is outside
bearing wall at right; effect of low ceiling
is less claustrophobic thanks to window
opening. Design: MLA/Architects.

In the Woods

Varying frame size of stair-step windows creates ever-changing woodland
vista. Transitional spaces are open; sitting areas have more privacy. Glazed
roof ties it all together. Interior double-hung windows up high tap warm air
that rises in solar-effective space, direct it to rooms on other side of house.
Architects: Moore Grover Harper.

On the Water

Corner windows soaring two stories allow panoramic view from both living room and balcony bedroom. Awning windows above and below admit cooling breezes; pole opens upper ones. Architects: Repass & Fulton.

High on a Hill

Delicate stained-glass tracery framing dramatic vista from hillside dining room enhances sense of enclosure without disrupting view. Because Craftsman style of house precluded large plate-glass windows, series of double casements was used instead. Architects: Abrams, Millikan & Kent of Berkeley.

LIGHT FROM ABOVE, LIGHT FROM THE SIDE: IDEAS TO BRIGHTEN YOUR COMINGS & GOINGS

Friendly Alliance
New and old meet in entry to high-ceiling master-bedroom suite. Small-paned casement and door echo traditional style of house; large fixed pane is frankly modern. Combination is striking, yet unexpectedly harmonious. Architect: Peter C. Rodi/Designbank.

Urbanity Updated
Sleek entry makes good use of glass blocks, yesterday's sophisticated building material. Blocks brighten entry without sacrificing security. Fixed glass in and above door strikes modern note. Architect: Ted T. Tanaka.

Sculptural Treatment
Skylight added to bring light into east-facing entry extension features distinctive detailing. Sculptured "shaft" complements shape of skylight, adds height, eases transition from ceiling to sky. Pair of plate-glass windows framing door gathers additional light. Architect: John Galbraith.

Uncluttered Elegance
Potentially dark lower-floor entry gains light from lavish use of glass. Custom-built door interrupts rigorous geometry of windows. Concrete post (reflected in window to left of door) supports overhanging story. Architect: Fred Briggs.

Twining Finery
Stylized vine in beveled glass enriches traditional doorway. Upper panels open inward for ventilation. Subtle use of stained glass adds touch of color. Design: Michael Felix.

LUMINOUS ALCOVES FOR DINING & DAYDREAMING, SITTING & SUNNING

Top-floor Library

Filled with light from high windows, cozy nook is ideal location for reading or just daydreaming. Located at peak of shed-roof house, double-glazed windows retain heat. On warm days, bottom window slides open to vent air from house. Architect: Steve Dolim.

For Sunset Fanciers

Like a string of pearls, fanciful lights bedecking top of greenhouse windows provide soft illumination after the sun sets. Tinted glass above shades nook; window seats conceal storage space below. Casement at right opens to welcome sea breezes.
Architect: Obie Bowman.

Classic Features

Never out of style, small-paned bay windows have an irresistible charm. Full-length windows in this bay face east for sunny family breakfasts.
Architect: William B. Remick.

Wayside Retreat

New hallway cabinetry creates enough depth for light-filled window seat. Original steel-framed windows were refitted with leaded glass and faced with Spanish cedar to match cabinets.
Architect: Peter C. Rodi/Designbank.

Indoor Garden

Romantic window seat is focal point of bright, flowery bedroom. Small panes and soft pillows make it cozy. Casements open for ventilation.
Design: Woody Dike and L. W. Grady.

BLOCKS, BEVELS & SPLASHES OF COLOR MAKE WINDOW MAGIC

Interplay

Lively swirl of stained glass adds color and rhythm to entryway. Bold geometry of finely crafted door lends subtle counterpoint. Architect: Chris Abel. Glass design: Jos Maes.

Crystal Flowers

Beveled-glass motif, echoed in leaded-glass arch, ornaments small casement window. Aluminum frame ensures ease of installation, weathertight fit, and trouble-free operation. Design: Judith Sutter.

Wall of Light

Curving glass-block wall defining perimeter of dining room add-on gives diners impressionistic view of garden and floods room with light. Glass blocks are once again a popular building material, newly appreciated for thermal efficiency and security. Architect: Mark Millett.

Rush of Elegance

Cattails bloom on casement window. Ingenuous stained-glass design provides enough opacity at bottom for upper-level bathroom's privacy, transparency toward top for sky gazing. Architects: Abrams, Millikan & Kent of Berkeley.

Small Charmer

Beguiling window of translucent stained glass fits into modern casement frame. Window contributes light and privacy to bathroom; action of casement allows easy cleaning of both surfaces from inside. Design: Michael Felix.

GARDENING'S GOOD IDEA COMES HOME: POPULAR POPOUTS, MODEST TO MAGNIFICENT

Indirect Lighting
Glazed roof of north-facing kitchen greenhouse window extends view up and over neighboring houses, makes kitchen brighter. Screened awning windows provide ventilation. Architect: Fred Briggs.

Tree-top Vista
Curved-eave commercial greenhouse section enclosing deck off living room adds indoor space. Dark tile floor soaks up warmth by day, releases it at night. Motorized windows at top open to allow flow-through cooling on warm days. Tinted film applied to upper panels prevents excessive heat build-up. On cold days, weatherstripped sliding glass doors separate deck and living room. Architect: Donald K. Olsen.

Off the Shelf

Plants thrive in kitchen greenhouse window, standard item in many home improvement centers. Available in varying sizes, it's an attractive way to augment kitchen display space. Handle in center opens top for ventilation. Design: Curt Williams.

Standout Feature

Dramatic greenhouse section and clerestory windows provide shelter and illumination for much of house. Double glazing is thermally efficient. House design concentrates most glass in this and similar greenhouse section, to meet energy—and budget—requirements. Architects: Larsen, Lagerquist & Morris.

On the Corner

Greenhouse construction opens outside walls of corner kitchen to light, a scarce commodity on uphill side of tree-covered downslope lot. Cantilevered ceiling is supported on bearing walls behind camera. Architect: Jay Fulton.

Pretty—and Practical, Too

Glazed garden entry court extends indoor-outdoor living space in small, traditional house. Fanlight in glass gable adds decorative element appropriate to style. Greenhouse netting, tacked in place during summer to reduce heat build-up, is removed in winter to increase solar gain. Overhead fan circulates air. Design: Woody Dike and L. W. Grady.

Well, Why Not?

Delightful tub-greenhouse combination steals a bit of space from deck off master bedroom for a feeling of bathing *al fresco*. Mini-blinds assure privacy; steel post carries structural load. Architect: Rob Wellington Quigley.

Seamless Addition

Part of bedroom remodel, greenhouse section achieves integrated look through careful detailing. White-enameled aluminum frames harmonize with painted wood trim; installation was easy. Large sliding windows maximize view and ventilation. New stud-frame wall at right is carefully smoothed into existing wall, avoiding "add-on" look. Architect: William B. Remick.

Innovative Use of a Modern Material

Malleable polycarbonate glazing forms shed roof of kitchen greenhouse. Each panel is bent and capped with an aluminum extrusion; no water can enter between panes. Developed for impact resistance, polycarbonate is nearly unbreakable, makes greenhouse safe from stray baseballs and other falling objects. Double-glazed casements at bottom expand view. Architect: Peter C. Rodi/ Designbank.

WARM FRIEND OR DISTANT ACQUAINTANCE? KEEPING THE SUN AT HOME

In the Mountains
Country home is heated almost entirely by south-facing glazed wall. Double-glazed windows and clerestory admit low winter sun that's absorbed in insulated concrete floor. Stored warmth is re-radiated at night. Overhang above clerestory and roller shades on lower windows provide summertime shade. Architect: J. Alexander Riley.

By the Shore

Garage doors form movable window-walls in year-round seaside home. In summer, home's orientation excludes high-angle sun; doors open to breeze. In winter, low-angle sun heats brick floor by day; at night, stored heat warms room, substantially reducing utility bills. Architect: Rob Wellington Quigley.

In the Trees

Home designed for passive solar gain exploits wooded site with glazed roof sections. In winter, sun passing nearly uninterrupted through leafless trees warms interior. In summer, nature provides shading canopy, yet house is bright with filtered sunlight. Architects: Moore Grover Harper.

On the Coast

High heating bills motivated addition of two-story greenhouse to home in coastal forest. Even on overcast days, heavy tile floor soaks up warmth of sun through expanse of double glazing. Warm air circulates to top floor via balcony cut-out above. Wood stove supplements solar heat at night and during severe weather. Architect: Don Jacobs.

TURNING DOWN THE HEAT, MANAGING THE LIGHT

Ethereal Barricade
Svelte vertical louvers open and close like draperies, but adjust like horizontal blinds to modulate sun. Unobtrusive design complements modern decor. Architects: Batter/Kay.

Good Idea Updated
Neatly encapsulated mini-blinds fit between panes of double-glazed casements. They offer sun control, never need dusting. Design: William Young.

Looping Lines
Constructed like Roman shades for windows, light canvas shades glide down guide wires to shield greenhouse breakfast area. When not needed, they draw up behind beam. Architects: Abel & Wilkes.

Strong Medicine
Sturdy shutters set in barn-door tracks mount vigorous defense against sun's hot-climate barrage. Shutters can be easily operated from second-floor windows. Architect: William Turnbull.

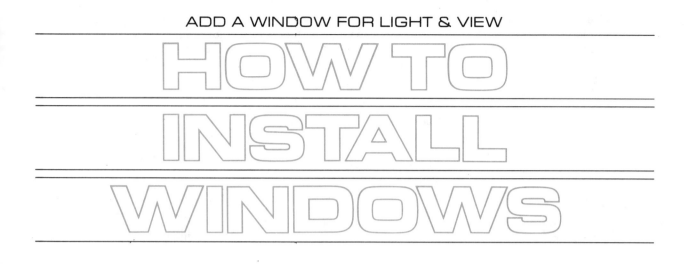

HOW TO INSTALL WINDOWS

Few do-it-yourselfers question their ability to replace an existing window with another window of the same size. But many may wonder whether they have the skills to cut a hole in the side of their house to add a window where there's never been one.

Actually, installing a window in a house with wood siding is fairly straightforward; only a knowledge of basic carpentry is required. But if your siding is masonry, masonry veneer, or aluminum, you'll probably need assistance from professionals. If you still want to do part of the job yourself, consult the *Sunset* books *Basic Masonry Illustrated* and *Do-It-Yourself Roofing & Siding* for information beyond the scope of this book.

You may also want professional help if you're installing a large expanse of glass; if the work involves moving pipes, wires, or ducts; if the new window is located within 4 feet of a corner of the house; if a bearing wall is involved; or if the job requires major structural changes. See page 22 for information on dealing with professionals.

Most windows sold through home improvement centers are ready-to-install prehung (prefabricated) units that come with frame, sash, glazing, weatherstripping, and hardware. Once you've removed the old window and prepared the opening, you can install such a window in a few hours.

In this chapter you'll find step-by-step instructions for installing several types of windows in a frame house. Instructions are given for using an existing opening, cutting a new opening, enlarging and reducing an existing opening, and closing an old one that's no longer needed. Be sure to read through all the procedures before you begin doing the work.

BEFORE YOU START

Taking a close look now at the wall you want to open will help you avoid problems—and perhaps added expense—later on.

Will work involve just one wall or will it require more extensive remodeling or redecorating? What type of framing was used in the construction of your house? Is the wall a bearing wall, that is, a wall at right angles to the ceiling joists or supporting rafters? Does opening the wall require any rewiring or rerouting of wires, pipes, or ducts (for information, see page 70)?

Are you required to have a building permit or conform to any building codes or regulations? Be sure to call your local building department and find out before you even begin planning.

Types of framing

How you'll shore up the ceiling before cutting the opening and how you'll frame it depend on the type of wood framing used in your house—balloon or platform (also called Western).

Balloon framing. Standard until about 1930, this framing is still used in some houses veneered with stucco, brick, or other masonry material. In balloon framing, the studs in bearing walls extend from the sill on top of the foundation up to the sill supporting the rafters.

From your basement or crawl space, examine the framing on top of the foundation. If the studs (usually 2 by 4s) rest on the sill and are nailed to the sides of the joists, balloon framing was used in constructing your house. Because of the length of the studs, you can't add new king studs for the opening; instead, you must use existing studs as king studs.

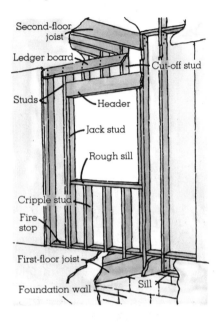

Platform or Western framing. Homes using this type of framing, common in residential construction for the last 50 years, are built in layers. The floor structure sits on

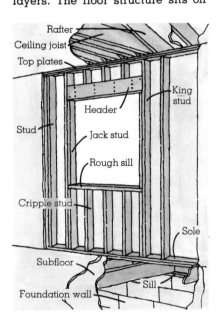

the foundation, and the first-floor walls follow on top of the floor. These walls support the ceiling and roof structures. In a two-story house, another floor and wall structure is built on the first-floor walls. In this type of construction, the studs are not visible from the basement or crawl space.

Bearing and nonbearing walls. You can add window openings to either kind of wall. But because the studs in a bearing wall support the weight of the structure above, the opening must be surrounded with heavy framing, and the ceiling above the opening must be supported while you're preparing the opening. Openings in nonbearing walls are much easier to frame and don't require shoring the ceiling.

To determine whether a wall is bearing or nonbearing, check the direction of the joists resting on a wall; they lie at right angles to a bearing wall and parallel to a nonbearing wall. Walls with eaves above them are bearing walls; walls under gables usually are nonbearing. If you have any doubt, check with an architect or your building department.

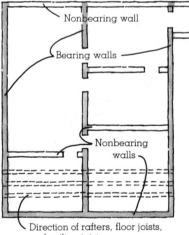

Anatomy of an opening

Before a window can be put in a wall, the opening must be framed with lumber to support the window; and if it's a bearing wall, the framing must also support the weight of

the structure above and transfer that weight to studs on either side of the opening.

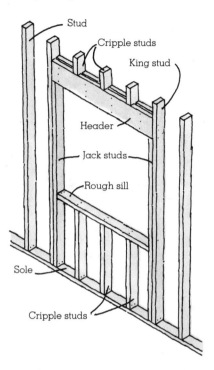

The rough opening size, the height and width of the opening for the window, is the measurement you'll work with in framing the opening with jack studs, header, and rough sill. Generally, these dimensions are ½ to 1 inch *larger* than the *actual size* specified for the window.

If you're replacing a window with a new one of the same size (see page 68), you'll need to measure the size of the existing rough opening. To do this, remove the trim from the inside of the window. Then select a window that calls for the same rough opening size.

Choosing your window

If you know exactly what kind of window you want, you can simply purchase it from you local home improvement center or order it from a manufacturer's catalog. But if you're not completely sure, you'll want to review the basic window styles described in the planning chapter that starts on page 4, and thumb through the color gallery beginning on page 32.

Price should not be your only criterion. Consider also the quality of the merchandise and the reputation of the manufacturer. You'll be living with that window for many years.

Checking the size. Though you have a rough idea of the size window you want, you'll need to determine if that size is available from the manufacturer of your choice.

When you check available sizes in catalogs, you'll discover that at least three sizes are given for the width and height of each window—nominal or sash size, actual or unit size, and rough opening size.

Nominal or sash size refers to the width and height of the sash inside the frame. This is the dimension that relates to the size you arrived at in your planning.

Actual or unit size is the measurement from the outside of one jamb to the outside of the other, and from the top of the head jamb to the bottom of the sill. This size includes the frame around the window.

Checking the wall. Don't make any final decisions on window size until you've located the window studs (see "Marking the opening," page 69). You may be able to simplify framing the opening by selecting a window slightly larger or smaller, or by moving the window to one side or the other.

After you've determined the window size and the size of the proposed opening, you're ready to purchase the window. Don't begin preparing the opening until you've received the window so you can check your measurements against the actual window.

Tools of the trade

If you're an active do-it-yourselfer, you'll probably have the tools needed to install a window with the exception of a reciprocating saw, which you can rent from a building supply or home improvement center.

Commonly used tools include
* steel tape measure or 6-foot folding rule;
* framing square to lay out the opening;
* combination square to mark the studs;
* two-foot or longer level to lay out the opening and make sure window and framing members are level and plumb;
* reciprocating saw to cut through wallboard, siding, sheathing, and studs;
* 16 and 20-ounce claw hammers to drive and pull nails;
* crowbar and pry bar to pull nails and remove siding, sheathing, studs, wallboard, and window;
* portable circular saw, table saw, radial arm saw, or crosscut

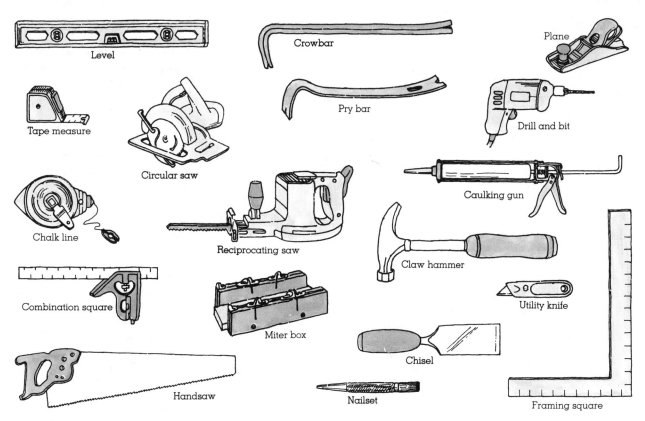

Level

Crowbar

Plane

Tape measure

Circular saw

Pry bar

Drill and bit

Chalk line

Reciprocating saw

Caulking gun

Combination square

Miter box

Claw hammer

Utility knife

Handsaw

Chisel

Nailset

Framing square

handsaw to cut framing, sheathing, siding, and trim;

- a miter box to cut trim;
- utility knife to score wallboard and cut tarpaper and caulking;
- tools to finish wallboard;
- wood plane (block or jack) to fit trim;
- pencil or chalk box to mark lines;
- caulking gun to seal joints.

Materials you'll need

In addition to the window itself, you'll need nails, lumber, and other materials to construct and finish the opening:

- 8, 10, and 16-penny common nails to frame the opening;
- 4, 6, and possibly 8-penny finishing nails to apply trim;
- molding, as required to trim the window;
- lumber to frame the opening;
- nails or screws, specified by the manufacturer, to attach the window;
- wallboard nails and materials to finish wallboard;
- caulking.

If you're not able to salvage enough sheathing and siding when you're cutting the opening, you'll have to buy more of these materials to finish the opening or cover a closed opening.

USING THE EXISTING OPENING

Installing a new window in an existing window frame is the easiest way to change a window. Replacing an old window and frame with one of the same size is not much more difficult. But you must remove the existing window and frame to expose the rough opening.

Before you remove the existing window, carefully pry off the trim from the inside of the window. Measure the size of the rough open-

ing and order a window that calls for the same rough opening size. When you have the new window, check to be sure it's the correct size.

Take out the sash, if possible, before removing the frame. On casement or awning windows, remove the operator (see page 92) and unscrew the hinges. With a sliding sash, lift the slider and pull it out from the bottom.

Removing the sash of a double-hung window is a little more complicated. Pry off the stop (see page 87), and then remove the lower sash and disconnect the sash balances. Pull out the parting strip (see page 88) and repeat with the upper sash.

Using a utility knife, cut through the caulking between the outside of the window and the siding. Use a crowbar, chisel, and hammer to pry off the trim around the outside of the window. Don't try to save the trim if your new window includes it.

Determine how the window frame is fastened to the house. It may be nailed directly into the framing around the opening or nailed to the framing or sheathing through flanges or brackets. Either pry out the nails with a crowbar or cut them with a hack saw. If the frame is nailed through a flange to the sheathing, pry on the frame to pull out the nails. If you're not planning to reuse the frame, saw through the sill and pry off the two pieces. Then remove the side jambs and head jamb.

Remove the window from the opening, pry out any exposed nails, and clear away the debris. To install the new window, see page 76.

OPENING THE WALL

Though a professional can install a window where none existed before in one day, it will probably take you longer. Plan to spread the work over several days, or even several weekends. The procedure described below allows you to keep

the exterior of your house intact until you're ready to put the new window in place.

The installation instructions on page 76 are typical; if they're different in any way from the manufacturer's instructions, follow the directions that came with your window.

Locating the opening

Illustrated on the next page are the different kinds of framing situations encountered in locating a window opening. Our instructions use an existing stud for one king stud and a new stud for the other. Adjust the procedures to meet your situation. If your house has balloon framing (see page 65), you'll have to use two existing studs as king studs. After the header is installed, use as many jack studs as needed to reduce the opening width to the correct size.

Finding the studs. To locate the studs on both sides of the opening, measure the actual width of the window (width over the outside of the jambs) and mark this width on the wall where you want the window.

Tap along the wall away from each mark and parallel to the floor; when the hollow sound changes to a dull thud, mark that spot. If your wall is covered with wallboard, you can use a stud finder instead, a magnetic device that indicates the positions of the nails holding the wallboard to the studs.

Find the *inside* edges of the two studs by tapping an 8-penny finishing nail into the wall (above the baseboard) where you think the stud is until the nail hits solid wood.

Work back toward the window opening until you locate the inside edge of the stud. Using your level to mark the edge of the stud, make a vertical pencil line on the wall. Repeat for the stud on the other side.

Reevaluate the position of the window. If moving the window a couple of inches allows you to use one of the studs you found as a king stud, you'll save considerable work.

FRAMING FOR WINDOW OPENINGS

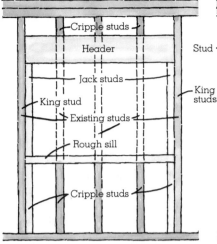

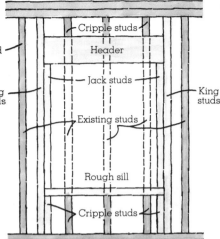

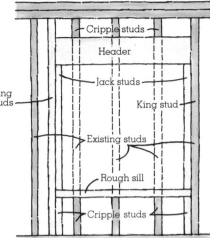

Window opening framed with two existing studs used as king studs.

Window opening framed with two new king studs.

Opening framed with new king stud and existing stud used as king stud.

Making a drawing. To avoid mistakes, it's a good idea to make a drawing of the existing framing. Then, with a pencil of a different color to keep the marks straight, sketch in the outline of the rough opening and the new framing (see drawing below). Mark all dimensions. Check them carefully and recheck them often as you work.

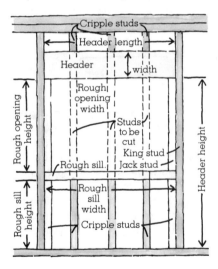

Marking the opening. With drawing in hand, you're ready to mark the wall area that you'll be removing. When you're using an existing stud for one king stud and installing a new stud for the other, you'll need to remove the wall covering from floor to ceiling between the king studs so you can nail the new stud to the sole and plate. If

you're using existing studs as king studs, you remove the wall covering from the bottom of the rough sill to the top of the header (see drawing above).

Using a level and a pencil, extend the line marking the edge of the stud (the one you're using for the king stud) up to the ceiling and down to the floor. Make sure it's plumb. Mark the location of the new king stud (as shown on your drawing) on the top and bottom of the wall by measuring from the line. Mark these points on the wall. Connect the two points on the top and the two on the bottom with straight, perpendicular lines. Check them with your level. Crosshatch the areas of the wall you need to remove.

If you're using two existing studs for king studs, you'll have to draw two horizontal lines to indicate the top and bottom of the wall covering to be removed. For the top line, measure down from the ceiling on one of the vertical lines the distance to the top of the header; mark this point. Using a level and a pencil, draw a horizontal line through this point to the other vertical line.

From the two corners, measure and mark the distance from the top of the header to the bottom of the rough sill, as shown on your drawing; connect these points with a horizontal line. This line marks the

lower edge of the wall area to be removed. These horizontal lines also indicate where the studs are to be cut to accommodate the header and the rough sill.

Marking the studs. You'll have to remove the wall covering before you can mark cutting lines on the studs you need to remove and mark the rough sill and header locations on any studs you'll use as king studs. *Shut off the power to any electrical circuits in the room before cutting.* Using a reciprocating or keyhole saw, cut along the vertical lines or the vertical and horizontal lines, as appropriate. Use a hammer and crowbar to remove the wall covering. Also remove any insulation in the wall. If any wires or pipes cross the opening, you'll have to reroute them (see next page).

(Continued on page 72)

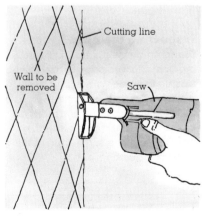

The smooth skin of your walls and ceiling may conceal wires, pipes, and heating or air-conditioning ducts just where you want to place that new window or skylight. If your detective work uncovers one of these obstructions, you can either change your plan for the location of the opening (at considerable savings of time and money) or reroute the offending object.

Though you may be able to reroute electric wires, water pipes, and round ducts yourself, leave rectangular ducts and steam, gas, or sewer pipes to professionals who have the specialized skills and tools required for the job. Since this work may be regulated by your local building code, check with your building department before beginning.

Finding hidden wires, pipes, and ducts

Unless you have a set of architect's drawings for your home, you'll have to search for some obvious, and some not-so-obvious, clues to obstructions that may lurk in the attic or wall.

Inspecting the attic. If you're planning a skylight, mark the ceiling opening (see page 98) and climb up into the attic with a light, tape measure, pencil, and paper. Locate the nails marking the ceiling opening corners and make a sketch of any obstructions in the area of the proposed opening.

Inspecting the wall. To find obstructions in a wall, either you or a professional must do some keen detective work. Look in the Yellow Pages under "Pipe Locating" to hire a specialist in locating wires and pipes.

If you're doing the job yourself, first make a sketch of the wall; be sure to show the position of the nearest side wall. Then, as you find clues to what lies behind the wall (see below), you can mark them on the sketch.

Here's what to look for:

• Take a look outside for any pipes coming through the roof directly above the proposed window opening. Pipes projecting above the roof indicate drain pipes in the wall directly below; you may find hot and cold water pipes, as well.

• Check the second story above the proposed opening; is there a radiator against the wall? If so, there may be a hot water or steam heating pipe in the window area.

• Is there a hot-air register in the wall under the proposed opening or above it on the second floor? If so, a heating duct may be in the wall. Remove the register's grill and reach into the duct to determine if it leads to the proposed window area.

• On your sketch, mark the locations of receptacles, switches, and wall lights. Connect them to reach each other with vertical and horizontal lines. Since electricians usually install wiring in these directions, the lines on your sketch show possible locations of wires.

• Go up in the attic with a light, tape measure, pencil, and your sketch. Locate the plate on top of the wall above the proposed window opening. Measuring from the nearest side wall (you should be able to see the top of it), mark on your sketch the locations of any wires, pipes, or ducts coming through the plate. If your house has a basement or crawl space, repeat the process.

When you've marked all this information on your sketch, you should have a good idea of the locations of wires, pipes, and ducts hiding in the wall. For definite confirmation, you can cut several 4 to 6-inch square holes in the area of the proposed opening so you can look and feel inside the wall. *Caution: Shut off the electricity at the main panel before you cut the holes.*

Sawing and drilling through framing. To relocate wires and pipes, you may need to notch or bore through joists or studs outside the area of the proposed opening. Consult your building department for any code requirements relating to notching or making holes in framing; often, such framing has to be reinforced.

Rerouting electric wires

Be especially cautious when working with electric wires. *Before touching the wiring, shut off the power at the main breaker.*

To reroute wires, cut them where they cross the opening. Then, making the connections in junction boxes (see drawing), connect each cut end to one end of an additional length of wire; twist the bare ends of the wires together and cap them with wirenuts. Last, install the covers of the boxes.

Identifying and rerouting pipes

If the pipe is 2 to 4 inches in diameter and made from copper, gray galvanized steel, black plastic, or black cast iron, it's probably a vent or drain pipe for the main plumbing system. Since the building depart-ment probably does not allow these pipes to be rerouted, you'll have to move the proposed window opening to avoid them.

A pipe that's ¾ to 1 inch in diameter and made from copper, plastic, or gray galvanized steel probably carries water through your main plumbing system. It must be emptied (see right) before work can begin.

A gas pipe is usually ¾ to 1 inch in diameter and made from black steel. If the pipe is galvanized steel or rigid copper and is wrapped in insulation, it's probably part of the hot water or steam heating system. Both types are best rerouted by a licensed plumber.

Emptying water pipes. Before cutting into a water pipe, you'll need to shut off and drain the water system. To do this, shut off the main valve where the water supply enters the house. Shut off the gas or electricity to the water heater. Then open an outside hose bib and all the inside faucets to allow the pipes to drain.

Rerouting a water pipe. Remove the section of pipe crossing the opening and reconnect the ends with pipes and elbows, as shown in the drawing. Building departments require use of the same material as the existing pipe.

Relocating air ducts

Because of the complexity of the work, rerouting rectangular ducts is a task for a professional. But you can easily extend round ducts that lie above the ceiling or under the floor, provided there's room to work. *Before you start, shut off the furnace or air conditioner.*

Remove as many sections of duct as necessary by unscrewing them at their joints. At each open end, add a 90° galvanized elbow; make sure the open ends point to the same side of the opening. Connect the elbows with one or more lengths of flexible aluminum or plastic duct, or with rigid galvanized duct (with rigid duct, you'll have to add two more elbows). Secure each joint with three sheet metal screws and seal with duct tape.

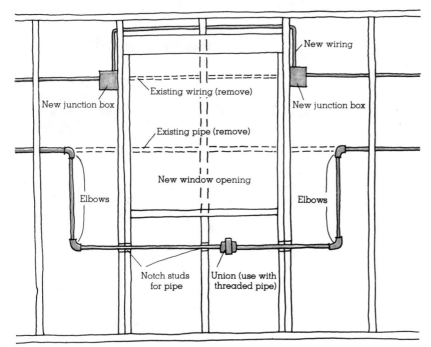

New wiring

New junction box

New junction box

Existing wiring (remove)

Existing pipe (remove)

New window opening

Elbows

Elbows

Notch studs for pipe

Union (use with threaded pipe)

. . . *Continued from page 69*

Referring to your drawing and measuring from the floor, mark the height of the bottom of the rough sill on each stud. Using a combination square and a pencil, mark horizontal lines through these points on two adjacent sides of each stud. On any stud you'll use as a king stud, mark a horizontal line on the side facing the opening.

Again referring to your drawing, similarly mark the height of the top of the header on each stud. If the top of the header is within 3 inches of the bottom of the plate, plan on removing the studs from the sill to the plate; make the header wide enough to set against the bottom of the plate. This will save quite a bit of work.

Do not begin cutting until you've supported the ceiling and structure above the marked opening.

Supporting the ceiling

The weight of the ceiling can cause even a nonbearing wall to sag or collapse unless you add extra support for the ceiling before you begin cutting through the studs. If your house was built with balloon framing, you'll have to provide additional support for the studs above the opening.

Building the ceiling support. To support the ceiling, you need to build a temporary wall slightly longer than the width of the opening and parallel to the wall. To allow enough room for working on the opening, erect the temporary wall about 4 feet away from the existing wall.

For a sole and plate, you'll need two 2 by 4s one to two feet longer than the width of the planned opening. To protect the flooring, use a piece of ½-inch plywood about 12 inches wide and slightly longer than the 2 by 4s. You'll also need enough 2 by 4s for studs, one at each end and one every 16 inches center to center. Mark the locations for the studs on the sole and the plate with a combination square and a pencil.

Measure the height from floor to ceiling and cut the studs to this dimension, minus 4 inches.

Position the plywood where you want the shoring wall and place a 2 by 4 for the sole on it. Nail the other 2 by 4 (the plate) to the ends of the studs with 16-penny common nails, two to each stud. Have your helpers erect the plate and studs on the sole; the plate goes against the ceiling. Toenail each stud to the sole with 8-penny common nails, two on each side.

While one of your helpers uses a level to make sure the wall is plumb on the side and the end,

2 by 4s

2 by 4s

Plywood strip   Shim

drive wedges between the sole and plywood until the plate is tight against the ceiling. Position shims under each stud.

Building the stud support. In a balloon-framed house, you need to support the studs above the opening, as well as the ceiling. You do this by placing a waler, a horizontal board, against the ceiling and bolting it to the studs. The waler must be long enough to span the opening and reach the studs beyond the king studs.

For the waler, cut a 2 by 8 at least 3 feet longer than the width of the rough opening if your studs are spaced on 16-inch centers, or about 5 feet longer if they're on 24-inch centers.

With a helper, place the waler on edge and hold it tight against the ceiling. Make sure the center is

over the center of the rough opening. Drive a few 10-penny nails through the waler into the ledger to hold it temporarily. Drill a pilot hole for a ½ or ⅜-inch lag bolt, at least 4½ inches long, through the waler and ledger and into each stud. Placing a flat washer under the head of each bolt, bolt the waler to the studs with the lag bolts.

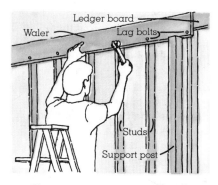

Ledger board

Waler   Lag bolts

Studs

Support post

For support posts, cut four 2 by 4s or two 4 by 4s long enough to wedge between the waler and the floor. Nail two of the 2 by 4s together with 10-penny common nails for one post and wedge it into position at one end of the waler. Repeat for the other end. Pad the ends, if needed, to protect the floor.

FRAMING THE OPENING

The frame you construct around the opening supports both your new window and, if it's a bearing wall, the ceiling above it. In this section you'll find detailed instructions for preparing the opening for the window.

Before you begin framing, gather all the materials you'll need for the job. Be sure to have on hand enough lumber for the king stud (if needed), the rough sill, the header, and the jack studs.

Cutting the studs

With a handsaw or reciprocating saw, cut the studs to be removed at the lines marking the bottom of the rough sill; be sure to cut exactly along the lines so the rough sill will fit tightly against the cripple studs.

Then cut on the lines marking the position of the header. Set the cut-off studs aside; you may be able to use them to build the framing.

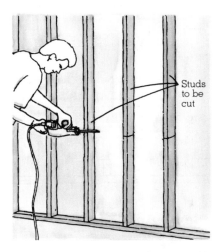

Studs to be cut

If your header fits tightly against the plate, remove the upper part of each stud completely. Remove any nails protruding from the plate.

Installing the king stud

Check your drawing for the distance between the king studs; measure and mark this distance from the existing king stud on the top of the sole and underside of the plate. Using a square and a pencil, mark a line through each point. On these lines you'll place the side of the new king stud that faces the opening.

Carefully measure the distance between the lines you just marked. Cut stud material to this length; make sure both ends are square. To set the stud in place, line up the face on the opening side with the top and bottom lines. Toenail the stud to the sole and plate with 8-penny common nails.

Installing the rough sill

Mark the height of the bottom of the rough sill on the sides of the king studs that face the opening. Measure down from these marks to the top of the sole and cut two cripple studs to these lengths. Use 10-penny common nails to fasten these crip-

ple studs to the facing edges of the king studs. Make sure the ends of the cripples fit tightly against the sole. The tops of the cripples should be the same height above the floor.

Measure the distance between the king studs across the cripples; cut a stud to this length for the rough sill. Place it on top of the cripples and toenail it to the king studs with 8-penny common nails. Secure it to the cripples with 16-penny common nails.

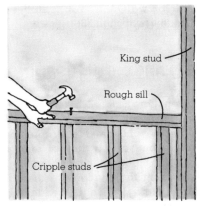

King stud

Rough sill

Cripple studs

Installing the header

In a bearing wall, the most important part of the framed opening is the header; it supports all the weight of the structure above the window. Even in a nonbearing wall, you'll need to install a header if you've cut any studs. The header fits between the king studs and is supported by jack studs at both ends.

The table below shows typical header sizes. But consult your local building department, an architect, or a structural engineer to determine the size required by code.

Maximum Span	Header Size
Feet	Inches
3½	Two 2 by 6
5	Two 2 by 8
6½	Two 2 by 10
8	Two 2 by 12

Unless a heavier header is required by your local building code, the header in a nonbearing wall is built in the same manner as the rough sill.

If your wall is framed with 2 by 4s, you'll need two pieces of framing lumber, each 1½ inches thick; check the building code for the correct width. The length of the header should be the same as the distance between the king studs. You'll also need ½-inch plywood the same width as the lumber to serve as a spacer between the two pieces of lumber. The plywood does not need to be one continuous length.

Some newer homes built for energy efficiency have walls framed with 2 by 6s to allow space for thicker insulation. If your wall is framed by 2 by 6s, you'll need three lengths of 1½-inch-thick lumber and two lengths of ½-inch-thick plywood.

If the top of the header will be within 3 inches of the ceiling plate, you can eliminate the cripple studs by making your header wider. The lumber will cost a little more, but you'll have less work to do.

If the span above the window is long, the space may not be wide enough for a header of the required width. In this case, you'll have to use a steel girder ordered from a structural steel company. Measure the required length accurately. Once the girder is cut, you can't adjust the length with your tools.

Assembling the header. Sight along the edges of the lumber to see if the pieces are curved. If so, assemble the header with the two crowned or convex edges on the same side; then install that side on top. Square up one end of each header piece and the plywood piece by marking them with your square and cutting them off with a saw.

Measure the space between the king studs where the header will be installed and check the measurement against your drawing. Make sure the measurements agree before you cut the lumber.

Starting from the squared-off end of each piece, measure to length and mark the point; draw a cutting line at that point with a combination square. Using a saw, cut each piece along the line.

Lay one of the 1½-inch-thick pieces on a flat surface; note the position of the crowned edge, if any. Place the plywood on top and cover it with the other piece of lumber. Make sure its crowned edge is on the same side as the first piece of lumber.

Line up the edges and nail the pieces together with 16-penny common nails, placing two nails at each end about 2 inches from the cut edge and staggering them about 12 inches apart along the length of the header. If the ends protrude through the other side, clinch them over.

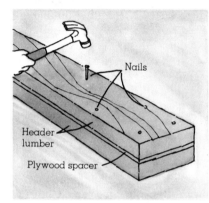

Installing the header and jack studs. Measure along the new king stud from the floor to the top of the header. Check that the mark is level with the mark on the other king stud.

Measure the distance from the top of the rough sill to these marks and cut stud material for jack studs to fit. If the header rests against the plate, toenail the header to it.

Have your helper position the top of the header, crown side up, against the cripple studs or plate while you place the jack studs against the king studs. Use a hammer, if necessary, to drive them into position against the king studs. Nail the jack studs to the king studs with 10-penny common nails. Be sure that the distance between the jack studs is the same as the width of the rough opening on your drawing.

The header should fit tightly against the sheathing on the outside and the cripple studs or plate

above it. If necessary, drive shims between the tops of the jack studs and the header until it fits tightly. Measure the distance between the bottom of the header and the top of the sill at each end and make sure it matches the height of the rough opening on your drawing.

Using 8-penny common nails, toenail the ends of the header to the king studs and the cripples to the header.

You can patch the interior wall now or wait until you install the window (see page 76).

ENLARGING AN OPENING

Often there's more work involved in enlarging an opening than in cutting a new hole in a wall. You have to take out not only the old window, but also much of the rough framing, including the header and the sill. And before you rip the header out, you must build a temporary wall to support the ceiling.

The methods used to enlarge an opening are similar to those for making a new opening; be sure to read "Opening the wall," pages 68–72.

Planning the opening

Remove the trim from around the inside of the window so you can study the framing (see the drawing of a typical framed opening on page 66). Make a drawing of the existing opening showing all the existing framing pieces.

Mark the rough opening for the new window on the drawing with a pencil of a different color to help you keep the measurements straight (see drawing above right). Then, with the same color pencil, draw in the new framing pieces. It's helpful to mark the rough opening size and the measurements for the header, rough sill, and jack and cripple studs.

From your drawing, determine how much wall covering you need to remove to build the new framing. Mark the outline of this area on the wall (see page 69).

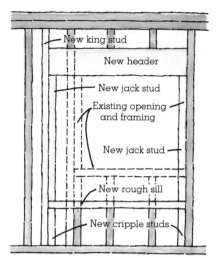

Removing the old framing

Using a reciprocating or keyhole saw, cut along the lines you marked on the wall (see page 69). Pry off the wall covering and remove any insulation behind it. If any wires or pipes cross the enlarged opening, they'll have to be rerouted (see page 70).

Build a temporary wall support (see page 72) to prevent the ceiling from sagging or collapsing. If your house was built with balloon framing, you'll also need to build a support for the studs above the enlarged opening. To determine the type of framing, see page 65.

Remove the window as described on page 68. Check the jack studs; if they run all the way to the floor, cut them flush with the top of the rough sill. Pry them away from the sides of the opening with a crowbar, remove the nails, and set the studs aside.

Pry out the header with a crowbar. If it doesn't come away easily, put a hacksaw blade in a reciprocating saw and cut through the nails holding the header. Since the sheathing on the outside is nailed to the header, you may have to remove some of the siding and sheathing to free the header.

Mark cutting lines on all the studs within the opening at the height of the bottom of the rough sill and the top of the header, as described on page 69. Cut the studs along these lines and remove the cut-off pieces and the rough sill. If you're cutting close to the bottom of the rough sill, remove the sill first and the nails holding it to avoid hitting a hidden nail with your saw.

Then remove any exposed nails from the remaining framing and clear away the debris.

Framing an enlarged opening

The procedure for framing the opening is essentially the same as that described for framing a new opening (see page 72).

Be sure to check the lengths of the cripple studs before installing them. Install the king stud; then cut and nail a cripple stud to it to support the end of the rough sill.

Build the new header and cut the jack studs to length. Install the header as described on page 73. Nail the jack studs to the king studs; then toenail the header to the king studs and the cripples to the header.

If any sheathing or siding overlaps the rough opening, use a saw to cut it back to the edges of the opening. To install the window, turn to the next page.

REDUCING THE SIZE OF AN OPENING

It's fairly easy to install a window that's smaller than the existing window. After removing the old window, you simply frame in from the sides of the existing opening. The hardest part of the job is finishing the framed area to match the siding outside and the wall covering inside.

Planning the opening

Remove the trim from the inside of the window. Make a drawing of the existing opening and mark its width and height.

Determine where you'll position the new window in the opening. Since the tops of the windows in a house are usually the same height, use the bottom of the header as the top of the new opening. Though you can center the window in the opening, you'll have less work if you use an existing jack stud for one side of the opening.

Framing the opening

Measuring from the existing jack stud, mark the width of the new opening on the top of the sill and the bottom of the header. Using a combination square, draw a line across the sill through this point. Repeat on the bottom of the header. On these lines you'll place the side of the new jack stud that faces the opening.

Cut a piece of stud material to fit between the header and the sill. Toenail this new jack stud to the header and sill with 10-penny common nails. Check the distance between the two studs at the top and bottom of the opening. This measurement should be the same as the width of the rough opening on your drawing.

If the new stud is close to the old jack stud, use several pieces of stud-width lumber to form the side of the new opening. Measure the distance between the new stud and the old jack stud on that side of the opening. If it's more than 14½ inches, install additional studs between header and sill to fill that space; they should be 16 inches center-to-center or 14½ inches apart.

To install a new rough sill that's 3 inches or less above the existing one, nail layers of stud-width material to the old sill to form the bottom of the new opening. Measure the distance between the header and the new rough sill on both sides of the opening. These measurements should be the same as the height of the rough opening on your drawing.

If the new rough sill is considerably higher than the old, don't try to build it up. Instead, use 10-penny common nails to toenail another set of cripple studs to the existing sill. The length of the new cripples should be the same as the distance between the top of the old sill and the bottom of the new one. To make the rough sill, cut a piece of stud material the same length as the width of the rough opening and nail it to the top of the new cripples with 16-penny common nails.

Finishing the opening

Patch the sheathing on the outside. Using 8-penny common nails, secure stud material to the existing framing to support the edges of the new sheathing, if necessary. Patch the siding after you install the new window.

Fill the spaces between the new and old framing with insulation, vapor-barrier side facing in. Replace the wall covering around the opening. To install the window, turn to the next page.

OPENINGS FOR SPECIAL WINDOWS

Bays or oriels, bows, greenhouse, and most other special windows require rectangular openings framed in the same manner as shown in the drawings on page 69. But be sure to study the manufacturer's instructions carefully for any special requirements. Some bay windows, for example, extend from floor to ceiling and require substantial structural changes best left to a contractor.

Difficult to frame are those special windows with nonrectangular shapes—circular, semicircular, quarter-circle, hexagonal, and octagonal. With each of these, you first frame a square or rectangular opening with header, jack studs, and rough sill (see page 66). Then you must add additional framing to support the window (see drawings on page 76). Framing should be no closer than ½ inch to the outside of the window frame.

To install the window, see the next page.

INSTALLING A WINDOW

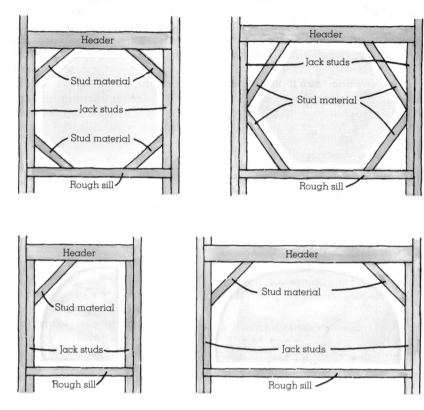

CLOSING AN OPENING

Removing an existing window and closing the old opening is easy; what's difficult is matching the new surfaces to the old ones, both inside and outside.

Installing the framing

Remove both the interior and exterior trim; then lift out the window from the opening (see page 68). Be careful not to damage the window if you plan on using it again. Remove all exposed nails and fastenings, and clean up the debris.

Measure the width of the studs. If they're wider than standard lumber (3½ inches for 4-inch-wide lumber and 5½ inches for 6-inch-wide lumber), you'll have to buy wider material and saw it to the required width for the studs you need to frame the opening.

Measure the distance between the sill and the header. Cut enough studs to enclose the opening: one on each side of the opening and one every 16 inches center-to-center or 14½ inches apart within the opening. Nail one stud to each existing jack stud with 8-penny common nails. Toenail the rest of the studs to the header and sill with 10-penny common nails. Space them 16 inches center-to-center or 14½ inches apart.

Finishing the wall

Cover the outside with sheathing; using 8-penny common nails, secure stud material to the existing framing to support the edges of the new sheathing, if necessary.

Apply siding or other material to the sheathing to match the existing material. Finish the siding so it blends with the existing finish.

Fill the open spaces between the framing members with insulation, vapor-barrier side facing in. Apply wallboard, paneling, or other material to the inside of the closed opening to match existing material.

Whether you cut a new opening, enlarge or reduce an existing one, or use the old opening, the directions for installing the window are the same. The only difference is whether the window is prehung (includes the frame) or is designed to be installed in an existing frame. Take note of the method of installation recommended by the manufacturer. Since these methods vary from one manufacturer to another, be sure to study and follow these instructions.

Described below are typical methods for installing a prehung window and frame in a rough opening, a metal window in an existing frame, a bay or bow window, a greenhouse window, and a nonrectangular window in a frame.

Installing a prehung window

A prehung window comes complete with sash, frame, sill, hardware, and all the trim, except for the casing, stool, and apron which you must supply. The window can be double-hung, casement, or awning and may be made from vinyl, wood, or vinyl or aluminum-clad wood.

It's easiest to install this window from the outside, though you can maneuver it through the opening from the inside and lean through the window to fasten it.

Cutting the outside opening. If you're putting a window in a new opening, you're ready to cut away the sheathing and siding. From the inside, drill a hole through the sheathing and siding at each corner of the rough opening. Stick a nail through each hole so you can find the holes on the outside.

On the outside, mark the outline of the rough opening on the siding with a pencil and level (as shown in drawing) or a straightedge (a long 1 by 4 or 1 by 6). Or stretch a chalk line around the four nails and snap it between each pair.

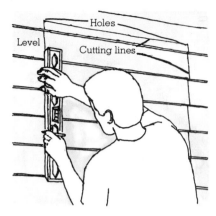

Using a reciprocating or circular saw, cut through the siding and sheathing along the lines and lay the cut material aside.

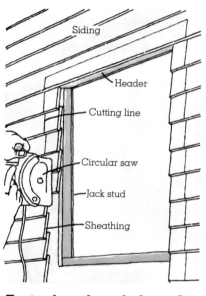

Fastening the window. One method of attaching a prehung window is to nail through a flange that surrounds the window and sets against the sheathing. Another method is to nail through the trim on the outside of the window into the sheathing. A third way is to screw the jambs to the jack studs and header. The method used is determined by the manufacturer.

If necessary, assemble the mounting flanges and flashing of your window according to the manufacturer's instructions.

Center the window in the opening and have your helper hold it in place; use a level to check that the head jamb is level. Using a pencil, mark the outside of the flange on the

siding and remove the window. Carefully remove enough of the siding to clear the flange area.

If the window is fastened through the exterior trim or the jambs, carefully plumb and level the frame while your helper holds

the window firmly against the side of the house. Use a pencil to mark the outside of the window trim on the siding, then remove the window. Using a circular saw with the blade set to cut through the siding but *not* through the sheathing, cut along the marked lines; discard the siding. Set the window back in the opening, level and plumb it, and nail through the outside trim or jamb.

Center the window in the opening again while your helper holds it in place. Drive a 6-penny common nail through the flange on top near one of the corners. Checking with your level, use wood shims to level the top jamb and plumb the side jambs. As an additional check, use a framing square to make sure the corners are square. Spacing the nails about 8 inches apart, finish nailing the top flange.

Maintain a constant width at the top center and bottom by using shims between the jambs and jack studs. Starting at the center of each flange, nail them to the sheathing, spacing the nails 8 inches apart.

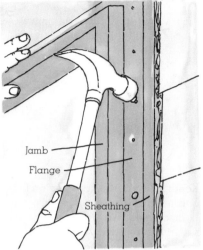

Most manufacturers recommend installing the trim on the inside of the window (see page 82) before removing any blocking or bracing installed to prevent damage during shipment. After you've trimmed the window, remove such material and check that the sash operates freely.

Finishing the outside. Unless your roof has a pronounced overhang, your local building code may require flashing over the top of the window. Check with your building inspector.

Covering any exposed sheathing with tarpaper, replace the siding around the window. You'll find information on installing various types of siding in the *Sunset* book *Do-It-Yourself Roofing & Siding.* Thoroughly caulk the joints between the siding and the new window.

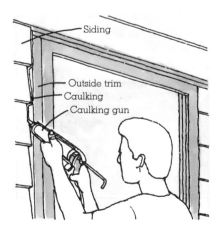

Keeping would-be intruders on the *outside* is an important concern for homeowners. Ways to ensure your security and privacy include adding locking devices to make windows and sliding glass doors difficult to pry open; replacing ordinary glass with tempered, laminated, or wire-reinforced glass or with plastic; attaching grilles to windows; and installing perimeter alarm systems.

Locking tips

Available on the market are dozens of ready-made devices that make prying open a window or sliding glass door more difficult; home-made devices may be even more effective. The type of locking device you choose depends on the type of window—sliding, double-hung, or casement.

Sliding windows and doors. Sliding panels present a major security problem because they can be lifted off their tracks.

To keep a sliding sash or door from being lifted out, insert three sheet metal screws, evenly spaced, into the groove of the upper track. Adjust the screws so they just fill the space between the groove and the top of the door or sash, making it impossible to lift out.

The easiest way to keep an inside panel from sliding is to drop a dowel or piece of tubing into the empty portion of the lower track. Cut the dowel or tubing ¼ inch shorter than the distance between the panel and the jamb.

Manufactured track grips, tightened by a thumb screw or key, are metal stops that straddle the lower track and secure inside panels. A spring bolt lock has a pin that snaps through a hole drilled in the edge of the lower track and bottom of the sash. Use this lock on either inside or outside panels.

Double-hung windows. You can buy wedge locks, key-operated cam latches, and pin locks to secure double-hung windows.

To create an even more secure lock for a wooden double-hung window, drill holes that angle slightly downward completely through the top corners of the bottom sash and halfway into the bottom corners of the top sash. A loosely fitting eye bolt acts as the lock—the eye makes a handle for removing the bolt.

Casement windows. The existing hardware on crank-operated casement windows is usually adequate to keep the windows closed, but you can buy cranks that lock.

Break-resistant window panes

Making window panes difficult to cut through or break strengthens the defense against intruders.

Tempered glass (it crumbles, rather than splinters, when broken) is five times stronger than ordinary glass. Laminated glass (plastic laminated between two panes of glass) is even stronger and increases the difficulty of cutting; so

does the steel mesh embedded in wire-reinforced glass.

Replacing the glass with acrylic or polycarbonate makes the pane almost unbreakable, but plastic has a few disadvantages: extra cost, the likelihood of scratching, and a tendency to yellow after a few years. See page 15 for information about using glass blocks in place of panes.

Window guards

Perhaps the surest way to keep intruders out is to install a grille across the outside of a window. Unlike a lock, a grille allows a secured window to remain open for ventilation. But be sure to equip each grille with an inside escape lever linked to the grille through a hole in the wall. One push on the lever releases one side of the grille from its mount and allows the grille to swing open.

Perimeter alarm systems

Installing an alarm system that links windows and doors to a central bell or horn can be a very effective method of securing your home. In one system that's commonly used, two-part magnetic contacts placed on windows and doors are wired into the household electrical system. When an opening is forced, the two parts separate, breaking the current and sounding the alarm.

Investigate several different systems before deciding on one for your home. Look in the Yellow Pages under "Burglar Alarm Systems."

Installing a metal window in an existing frame

Some prehung windows, usually single or double-hung and made from aluminum, can be installed in existing wood double-hung or casement frames. Using an existing frame eliminates the work of framing the rough opening and patching the interior and exterior surfaces around the window.

You'll need to remove the existing sash, hardware, stops, and parting stips from the frame. Installing the new window is an easy job, but be sure to consult the manufacturer's directions for your particular window. Don't begin until you have the new window; measure the height and width of the outside of its frame to make sure it fits properly inside the existing frame.

Preparing the frame. To remove a single or double-hung window, pry off the inside stop and remove the lower sash and balance. Then pull out the parting strips to remove the upper sash and balance (see page 88).

If you're replacing a casement window, remove the operating hardware (see page 92) from the sash and stool, and the latch from the frame. Pry off any stops nailed to the jamb. Then unscrew the hinges and remove the sash.

If you're planning to paint any part of the old frame that will be exposed after the new window is in, you'll find it easier to do the preparatory work now.

Fastening the window. Aluminum windows (described below) are held in the existing frame with stops nailed on the inside and outside.

Following the manufacturer's instructions, nail stops on the side and top jambs. Set the window in place and secure it with stops nailed to the jambs as shown in the drawing. In a double-hung frame, you may have to remove the stool to install the window; replace it after the window is in place. Install any other stops or supports required by the manufacturer.

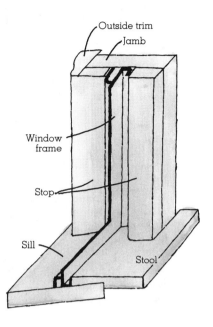

Installing a greenhouse window

Most greenhouse windows are designed to fit the most common window sizes (see page 14); they're fastened to the exterior wall of the house with the bottom of the window below the sill or resting on it. If you're installing a greenhouse window in a new opening, you'll have to frame a rough opening for it (see page 66). Be sure to follow the manufacturer's instructions for the opening.

Preparing the opening. Check the surface around the window. If it's flat and smooth, you can attach the mounting flanges of the greenhouse window directly to it. But if the surface is rough or covered with shingles or beveled siding, you'll need to cut back siding and install furring strips as shown.

Use ¾-inch-thick wood wide enough to extend beyond the mounting flanges. Set the furring strips in a generous bed of caulking; using nails long enough to penetrate the framing, fasten the furring through the siding and sheathing to the main structure of the house. Set the nails so they don't project above the surface of the furring strips.

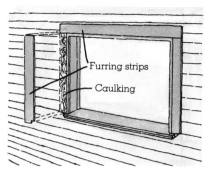

If you're using an existing window opening, strip the sash, stops, and interior trim from the window; leave on only the head jambs, sill, and exterior trim.

Fastening the window. Run a generous bead of caulking around the flange where it meets the furring strips. With some helpers, raise the window into place. While they hold it, attach the flange to the house with woodscrews long enough to go through the furring, siding, and sheathing, and bite into the house frame at least 1 inch.

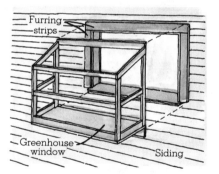

Run a neat bead of caulking around the joint between the flange and the furring.

To finish the inside, attach casing around the head and jambs (see page 82). Finish the bottom of the window with a stool made from wood or, if you're going to keep plants in it, with one made from ceramic tile.

Installing an octagonal window

Installing an octagonal or other nonrectangular window (see page 13) is not difficult, once you've framed the rough opening. What is difficult is trimming around the window on the inside. If you're not an experienced woodworker, you may want to have a cabinetmaker or other fine woodworker make the trim for you.

Though the method described below is for an octagonal window, it's applicable to round, hexagonal, and other shapes. If the outside of the window is exposed to the weather, you'll need flashing for the upper half. Have a sheet metal shop make the flashing for you; they can work from the window itself or from a sketch showing accurate dimensions.

Preparing the opening. At each corner of the rough opening, drill holes through the sheathing and siding. Mark the outline of the opening on the outside by connecting the holes with pencil or chalk lines. For a circular opening, locate the center of the opening and use it to mark the circle. Using a reciprocating saw, cut along the lines.

Fastening the window. If the siding is flat and smooth, the exterior trim can fit against the flat surface. Since you can't use flashing, be sure to run a generous bead of caulking around the trim where it meets the siding to weatherproof the joint.

If the siding is rough, set the window in the opening and mark the outline of the exterior trim on the siding. Saw around the lines and remove the siding.

Fasten the flashing, if used, to the window, setting it in a bed of caulking. Apply a bead of caulking on the back of the trim and on the flashing.

Put the window back in the opening and center it with shims between the jamb and the framing. Drive 8-penny galvanized finishing nails through the exterior trim and sheathing into the rough frame; predrill nail holes in the trim to avoid splitting.

Carefully caulk all joints between the window and the siding.

You'll find information on trimming the inside of the window on page 82.

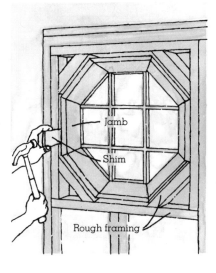

Jamb

Shim

Rough framing

Installing a bay or bow window

In the classic bay window design, the wall of the house projects to line up with the window. To add this type of bay to an existing house requires major structural changes best left to professionals. But the cantilevered bay, also known as an oriel, and the bow window (see page 13) can be built in the same type of opening as a conventional window. Though it involves more work than for a conventional window, installing one of these is no more difficult than installing any window in a rough opening, provided you have some helpers.

Depending on the manufacturer, a bay window may come as a kit with the windows, head board, and seat board (see drawing), plus various trim pieces you must assemble. Or you can buy a completely assembled unit ready to install. You simply build the roof over the window (unless it reaches the soffit), install support or knee brackets, and finish the inside. Some manufacturers even supply a precut roof and the support brackets.

The installation method described below is for a bay, but it's applicable to a bow, as well. Be

sure you have all the material that comes with the window before you start.

Preparing the window and opening. Unless you bought a completely assembled unit, assemble your window according to the manufacturer's instructions.

Check the outside dimensions of the window against the opening you framed in the wall. The height and width of the window should be about ½ inch less than the opening's height and width. Make any necessary adjustments.

Consult the manufacturer's instructions to see if you have to cut back the siding to clear the trim on the window. If so, mark the outline and cut along the lines with a circular saw. Set the blade to cut through the siding only.

To set the window in place, you'll need helpers, one for every 3 feet of window width. You'll also need a sawhorse every 3 feet to support the window once it's installed in the opening.

An assembled window is heavy and unwieldy. Installing one on the second floor requires strong scaffolding for a working platform. Unless you're experienced, have a professional do the installation. You can finish the interior yourself.

Fastening the window. Pick up the window and rest the bottom platform on the rough sill. Then tilt the unit up so the trim around the outside butts against the sheathing. Center the jambs between the

Rough opening

Window

Seat board

Sawhorse

jack studs. While your helpers hold the window against the siding, support it with sawhorses. Don't let your helpers leave; they'll come in handy when you level and plumb the window.

Use a level to determine which end of the seat board is the highest. Nail that end to the rough sill, placing the nail 2 to 3 inches from the jamb. Leaving the level on the seat board, drive shims between the sill and the seat board until the seat board is level; place the shims over each cripple stud. When the seat board is level, nail it through the shims to the sill.

Check that the jambs are plumb in two directions. To do this, put the level on the side of the jamb. While helpers move the window as needed (have one hold the level for you), drive shims between the jamb and the jack stud until the jamb is plumb. Space the shims about 12 inches apart and make sure the jamb is absolutely straight.

Placing the level on the interior edge of the jamb, move the top of the window in and out until the jamb is plumb. Check the side of the jamb again to be sure it's still plumb. Drive nails through the jamb and shims into the jack stud; be sure not to drive them through any part of the window mechanism. Repeat the process at the other hand.

Shim between the head board and header until the head board is straight. Measure at several places between the head and seat boards; the measurements should be exactly the same. Secure the head board by driving nails through it into the shims and header. Fill any spaces between the jambs and the framing with insulation.

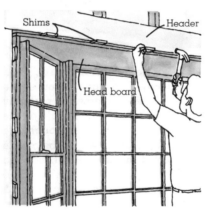

Install a drip cap around the top of window and any other exterior trim required.

Installing support brackets. If there isn't a cripple stud underneath each mullion, toenail one to the sill and the sole under each one.

Position one of the support brackets under one of the mullions with the long leg against the siding and the short leg against the underside of the window. Use ⅜-inch lag screws to fasten the long leg through the siding into the cripple stud. Fasten the other leg to the underside with woodscrews. Then install the other bracket.

If the manufacturer requires any brackets or supports between the head board and the studs above the window, install them.

Building the roof. Unless there's a soffit right above the window, you'll have to build a roof. Design it to reflect the architectural style of your home. The roof described below is one type that comes precut with a window. The method can be applied to most others.

Lay the center piece of the roof sheathing on the drip cap and against the siding. Mark the siding along the edge of the sheathing. Lay the end pieces in place and mark the siding where their edges touch. Remove the roof sheathing. Saw through the siding along the lines and pry it off.

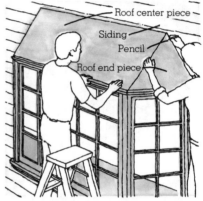

Nail the hip and end rafters at each end as shown. Nail the end pieces of sheathing to the rafters and to the top of the windows. Use 6-penny common nails spaced 6 inches apart. Cover the top of the head board with insulation; then nail the center piece of sheathing in place.

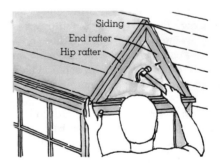

You can shingle the roof of the bay to match your house or have a professional cover it with copper. If you shingle the roof, you'll need flashing (see page 102) between the shingles and siding. Have the flashing made by a sheet metal shop. For more information on flashing and shingling, see the Sunset book *Do-It-Yourself Roofing & Siding.*

Check around the outside and caulk any joints between the window and the siding. You'll find information on trimming windows below.

If there's a soffit above the window, just fill in the space between the trim on the outside of the window and the soffit above with a piece of molding or wood.

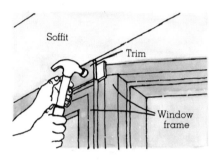

Soffit

Trim

Window frame

FINISHING THE INSIDE OF THE WINDOW

To complete the installation of the window, you'll need to finish the inside with molding. On a single or double-hung window, this involves fastening a stool to the window sill, attaching an apron to the wall underneath the sill, and fastening casing to the sides and top to cover the joints between the wall and window. Other types of windows—casement, awning, and hopper—are usually finished with casing on all four sides, though some makes require a stool and apron.

Tools you need. In addition to measuring tape, combination square, nailset, and hammer (see page 67), you'll need a miter box to help you cut accurate angles on the moldings, a fine-tooth (12 to 15 teeth per inch) miter saw for cutting the moldings, and a block plane for trimming moldings.

Head casing

Side casing

Jamb

Stool

Apron

Adding extension jambs to a window. In a modern house, the jambs on the window are probably flush with the inside wall of the house. In older homes, though, the edge of the jambs may be below the surface of the wall. You'll have to build the jamb out flush with the wall before you can put moldings on the window.

You'll need a piece of 1 by 6 clear pine slightly longer than the longest dimension of your window. If the window is wider than it is high, measure from the outside of one jamb to the outside of the other. If not, measure from the top of the head jamb to the bottom of the side jamb.

Set the edge of the board on the edge of the long jamb. Using a pencil, mark each end where it's flush

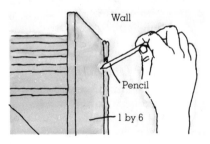

Wall

Pencil

1 by 6

with the wall. Remove the board and draw a straight line between the two points. Saw the board along the side of the line away from the jamb. Use finishing nails to attach the cut-off strip, sawed edge out, to the edge of the jamb. The nails should be three times longer than the sawed thickness of the strip. Repeat for the other jambs.

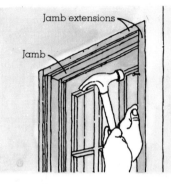

Jamb extensions

Jamb

If the extension jambs project beyond the wall or aren't flush with each other at the corners, countersink the nails in that area. Then plane the jamb flush. Toenail the extension jambs together at the corners with 6-penny finishing nails.

Trimming a double-hung window

To cut the stool, use a piece of the molding you'll use for casing and align one edge with the inside of the side jamb at the bottom. Draw a vertical line on the wall from about 2 inches above the sill to 4 inches below. Repeat on the other side of the window.

Using a miter box, square off one end of the stool and place it on one of the lines. Mark the other end of the stool where it crosses the other line, and saw this end square.

Place the stool so each end is lined up with the two lines on the wall, with the inside edge against the jamb; mark the stool for notching as shown on the drawings. Carefully cut the stool along the lines. Set the stool in place and fasten it to the sill with 6-penny finishing nails.

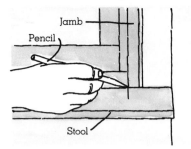

Position stool and mark inside of jambs on back edge of stool.

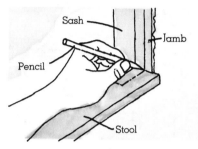

Place end of stool against jamb and back against sash; mark jamb face.

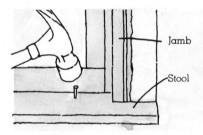

After cutting notch marked at each end of stool, nail stool to sill.

For the apron, cut a piece of molding 1 inch shorter than the stool. Position it under the stool so the ends are on the lines marked on the wall. Nail the apron to the sill with 6-penny finishing nails.

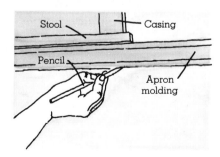

Aligning end of molding with end of stool, mark other end 1 inch shorter than stool.

Square off one end of a piece of casing molding. Set that end on the stool with the thin edge of the casing aligned with the inside face of the jamb. Mark the thin edge of the molding where the head jamb crosses it. Using the mitre box, cut that end at a 45° angle, making the thick edge longer than the thin edge.

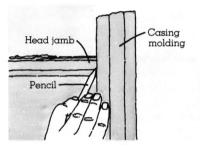

Setting molding on stool, mark head jamb on molding and cut it at 45° angle.

Set the casing back on the sill, align the edge with the face of the jamb, and nail it to the jamb with 4-penny finishing nails spaced about 8 inches apart. Then fasten it to the jack stud with 6-penny finishing nails. Repeat for the other side of the window.

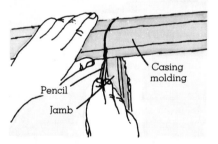

Placing molding across head jamb, mark side jambs and cut ends at 45° angle.

On another piece of molding, cut one end at a 45° angle for the casing across the top of the window. Fit that end into place before marking and cutting a similar angle on the other end. Nail the top casing to the header and head jamb.

Countersink all the nails and fill the holes with putty. Sand any rough areas before finishing the trim.

Trimming a casement window

If a stool is required, you'll trim a casement window the same way as a double-hung window (see above). For windows without stools, apply casing to all four sides of the window, mitering the ends of the casing at 45°. Nail the casing as described above.

Trimming a bay or bow window

A bay or bow window, whether double-hung or casement, is usually trimmed with casing on all four sides. If the seat and head boards are not included by the manufacturer, you'll have to cut and install them before applying the casing.

Trimming circular and nonrectangular windows

These windows are trimmed with casing on all sides; there's no stool or apron. But some of these windows present a real challenge to the do-it-yourselfer.

Circular windows. Unless you have a well-equipped wood shop, turn the making of casing for circular windows over to a cabinet-maker. You can nail the circular casing in place yourself.

Nonrectangular windows. Making the corner miter joint of a rectangular window is straightforward. For other shapes, you need to understand a little geometry. The angle at which you cut the casing must be half the desired angle of the corner. For an equilateral triangle, the angle you cut is 30°; for a pentagon, 54°; for a hexagon, 60°; and for an octagon, 67½°.

After you've cut the casing pieces and checked their fit, nail them to the jamb with 4-penny finishing nails and to the rough frame with 6-penny finishing nails.

Countersink the nails, putty the holes, and finish with paint or stain.

Creating a wall of glass in your home by adding glass doors serves a dual purpose: you can have all the benefits of a window with the added advantage of easy access to the indoors and outdoors. When oriented and designed for energy efficiency, glass doors let you enjoy natural light, provide solar heating benefits, and open your view of the outdoors without increasing your heating costs significantly.

Glass doors either slide or swing to open. Purchased partly or fully assembled, the doors include factory-glazed fixed and opening panels, assembled frames (including the threshold), factory-installed weatherstripping, hardware, and optional screens.

Designing glass door systems

Planning considerations for glass doors are similar to those required for window placement. The amount of heat and light entering through these doors is considerable, and so is the heat that can be lost; because of this, you'll want to give careful thought to the door's size, location, and glazing.

Wide door systems may require major structural changes in your home; if so, consult an architect or structural engineer.

Glazing. Both types of glass doors are available single glazed, double glazed for energy efficiency, or coated with a reflecting and heat-absorbing film. Most local building codes require that glazing for large expanses of glass in doors such as these be tempered for safety.

Combining the panels. Though both types of glass doors are most commonly used for access to patios, porches, and gardens, they can be entry doors, as well. To create glass walls ranging from a few feet long to the length of an entire wall—and even around the corner along an adjoining wall—you can arrange opening and fixed panels side by side in many combinations.

Sliding glass doors come in a number of combinations. Among the choices are two-panel units with one sliding panel, three-panel units with the center panel sliding, and four-panel units with the two center panels sliding. Several units can be installed side by side to create a window wall. Panel sizes can be 3, 4, or 5 feet wide and 6 feet 8 inches high. A few manufacturers offer 8-foot-high panels.

Swinging glass doors come as units of two or three panels; you can also purchase individual swinging and fixed panels and assemble your own combination. Panel sizes in this type of door are 2½ or 3 feet wide and 6 feet 8 inches high.

Sliding glass doors

Since the introduction of the original aluminum sliding patio doors of the 1950s, the sliding door system has evolved into an energy-efficient product in designs that fit most architectural styles. You can even buy a model closely resembling traditional French doors.

Materials for sliding glass doors. Sliding doors are made from aluminum (usually with a thermal break for energy efficiency), wood, vinyl-clad wood, or aluminum-clad wood.

Aluminum and vinyl-clad wood require the least maintenance; wood frames must be periodically refinished. On some wood sliding doors, the portions exposed to the weather are covered with aluminum that's finished with baked-on acrylic enamel.

Features of sliding glass doors. Because this type of door slides to one side, it doesn't require any clearance for opening either in the room or outside. Also, you can keep the door in any position from closed to fully open, and it will not move in a gust of wind.

With the proper hardware, you can lock a sliding door in a slightly open position. The opening can be narrow enough to prevent entry, yet allow some air circulation.

When security is a concern, you can obtain simple and inexpensive devices to secure sliding glass doors. To protect against a panel being lifted off the track, you can insert a few screws in the top groove. Of course, sliding doors, like all glass areas in a house cannot prevent the entry of determined intruders no matter which security device you install. Special security glass is available; though it's quite expensive, it is virtually breakproof.

When the sliding panel is on the outside of the fixed panel, you have good protection against the weather because the pressure of the wind seals the panel tightly against the weatherstripping.

Swinging glass doors

In the past, French doors had many drawbacks. Because they tended to warp and distort, they rarely fit well. They were difficult to weatherproof and impossible to secure.

Today's French doors have none of these problems. If the opening door is installed with one or more fixed panels, it has its own frame that can be weatherproofed and secured. When used in pairs, the doors are hinged on the sides and usually come together at a mullion in the center of the frame, a combination easy to weatherproof and secure.

Materials for swinging glass doors. You'll find these doors made from wood or steel-covered foam, materials with good insulating qualities for energy efficiency. Both wood and steel doors require periodic refinishing; if you care for the door on a routine basis, you won't find this difficult. The steel door is virtually free from warping and distortions.

Features of swinging glass doors. When mounted in pairs, most swinging doors close against a center jamb, rather than against each other as in the traditional French door. This allows better weatherproofing and security.

Because the rails and stiles of a swinging door are wider than those of a sliding door, the heat loss through the door is less than for a

sliding panel of equal size. Since a swinging door closes against side and top jambs, it can be better weatherproofed than a sliding panel.

For the same reason, better locks and security devices can be installed on a swinging door. Remember, though, that the door is only as secure against unwanted entry as the strength of the glass. A swinging door cannot be lifted off a track and removed.

Installing glass doors

Except for their greater size, sliding and swinging glass doors are no more difficult to install than windows.

As with a window, you can install the same size door in an existing opening, alter the opening for a larger or smaller door, or cut a new opening for a door.

Altering an existing opening or cutting a new opening is the same as for windows, except that the opening goes all the way to the floor. You locate the opening, support the ceiling, cut out the studs and sole, and install the header and jack studs (see "Opening the wall" on page 69). You do *not* install a rough sill or cripple studs under the sill.

Placing the door in the opening is also similar to installing a window (see "Installing a window" on page 77). Be sure to read the installation instructions accompanying the door and note the differences between window and door installation.

MAINTAINING & REPAIRING YOUR WINDOWS

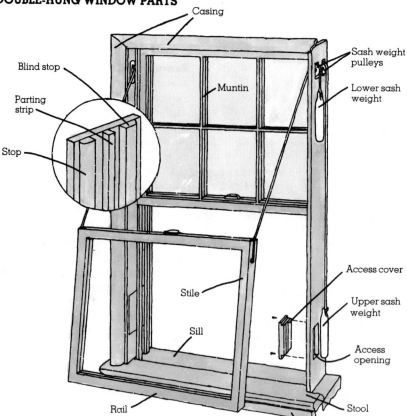

DOUBLE-HUNG WINDOW PARTS

Casing

Sash weight pulleys

Lower sash weight

Blind stop

Parting strip

Muntin

Stop

Access cover

Upper sash weight

Access opening

Stile

Sill

Rail

Stool

Apron

Movable windows are often beset with problems that hinder their smooth operation. A sash may stick or bind, or be so loose in its channel that it rattles; a sash balance or operator may need repairing; or a pane may need replacing.

Solving most of these problems requires only a few basic tools: chisel, hammer, screwdriver, pliers, utility knife, pry bar, putty knife, sandpaper, and finishing nails. Occasionally, you may need more specialized tools, such as clamps and a drill.

In the following pages you'll find detailed instructions for curing these and other common ailments of double-hung, casement, awning, and sliding windows.

DOUBLE-HUNG WINDOWS

Oldest of the various window types, the wooden double-hung (see drawing at right) often becomes troublesome with age. It may fit too tightly or too loosely in its frame because the sash or channels have swollen or shrunk with time; or it may stick or bind because layers of paint and dirt have built up between the sash and the frame. If a cord or balance is broken, the window may refuse to stay open in any position.

Freeing a stuck sash

If a sash is stuck temporarily, a change of weather may correct it. But if the window is paint-stuck, you can try to free it using one of the methods suggested below.

• To cut the paint seal, run a sharp utility knife between the sash and the stop molding on both sides of the window, and along the bottom between the sash and both the sill and the stool. Then use a wide putty knife to loosen the sash; tap the end of the knife with a hammer, if necessary.

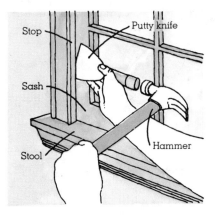

• If the window is closed, pry up the sash from the outside by wedging a pry bar between the sill and sash; work first at one end and then at the other to move the sash up evenly. Wood block protects sill.

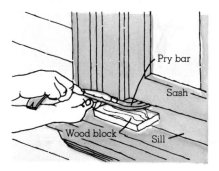

• If the window is open too wide to be pried, place a block of wood on top of the sash at one side, and tap down on it with a hammer. Alternate sides until the sash moves freely.

Easing a binding sash

Even after you free a sash, you may find that it moves reluctantly. It may be that the sash channels need cleaning and lubricating, or that a stop molding has to be planed and/or reseated to widen the sash track.

Cleaning the sash channel. Scrape off any paint or dirt that has accumulated in the window tracks, and sand all scraped surfaces. (Clean a metal or plastic track with steel wool.) Lubricate the tracks with household paraffin or commercial silicone lubricant; silicone spray works best for metal and plastic tracks.

Widening the channel. Sometimes the sash sticks against a jamb or a stop. Place a block of wood slightly larger than the channel at the point of binding, and tap the wood with a hammer against the stop until the channel is wide enough to allow the sash to move easily (see illustration below). If this doesn't work, you'll have to remove and reseat the stop.

Reseating the stop molding. To remove a stop molding, pry it away from the window frame with a chisel. (If the molding is fastened

with screws instead of nails, remove the screws first.) Minimize paint chipping by scoring the paint between the frame and the molding with a utility knife. If the old molding breaks during removal, save it to use as a sample when buying new molding.

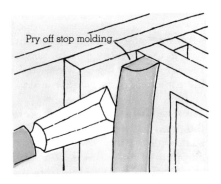

Before reseating the molding, chisel any built-up paint off the edge facing the sash, sand the stop and sash smooth, and apply paraffin.

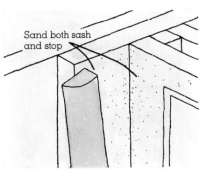

Reseat the molding. To give the sash added clearance, use a cardboard shim (a sheet from the back of a writing tablet works fine) inserted between the stop molding and the sash as a guide for the nailing. Fasten the molding to the frame with finishing nails.

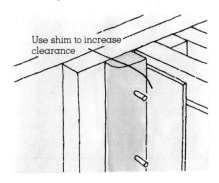

Fixing a loose sash

A sash that fits too loosely in its track rattles in the wind and lets in unwanted cold or warm air.

To remedy this problem quickly you can insert spring-type metal weatherstripping in the space between the stop molding and the sash. If the gap isn't too wide and the stop is nailed instead of screwed to the frame, another solution is to move the stop as shown below. If the gap is too wide, you'll have to remove and reseat the stop.

Moving the stop molding. Score the paint between the stop and the sash with a utility knife to prevent chipping. Then place a cardboard shim between the stop and the sash. Position a block of wood against the outer surface of the stop, and hammer toward the sash along the entire length of the molding until the paint breaks and the stop rests against the shim.

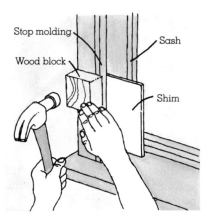

If the stop springs back to its original position, secure it in the desired position with finishing nails. Countersink and putty the new nails, and touch up the paint.

Repairing loose sash parts

Prolonged exposure to moisture can loosen glued mortise-and-tenon joints at the corners of a sash. Besides admitting water, loose joints can also make the sash jam.

To repair the loose parts, you'll have to remove the sash from the window frame. Take care not to break the glass.

To remove the lower sash, pry off the stop molding as described on page 87. Raise the sash enough to grasp it at the top and bottom, angle it toward you until it clears the frame, and slide it out.

Remove the knotted cords from the sash grooves. Untie the knots and release the cords; then tie larger knots or push a nail through the cords to keep the cords from feeding back into the pulleys.

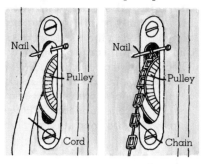

If chains hold the sash to the weights, immobilize the weights before detaching the chains from the sash. Draw up the chains until the weights touch the pulleys on both sides. Slip a nail through a chain link (see drawing above), and remove the screws or nails that hold the chains to the sash.

If your window has interlocking weatherstripping that fits into a groove in the sash, you'll have to remove it before you can free the sash from the frame. After removing a stop, raise the sash to the top and remove the nails that hold the weatherstripping to the track. Lower the sash and carefully angle the sash and the weatherstripping out of the frame.

To remove the upper sash, you first have to remove the lower sash. Using pliers, pry out the parting strip between the two sashes (see above right); protect the parting strip from the pliers by placing a piece of wood on both sides of the strip, or pull on a screw driven into the strip. Ease the upper sash out of the frame.

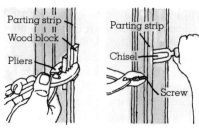

To reinforce loose corners, lay the sash on a flat surface and clean out the gap in the joint. If the sash is in good condition and the joint is clean and open, you can pour waterproof glue into the joint. Clamp it until the glue dries.

Another way to reinforce the corners is to drill holes and tap in glue-coated dowels. To do this, clamp the sash rails together. About ½ inch from the center of the adjoining rail, drill a ⁵⁄₁₆-inch hole into the stile about ¼ inch shorter than the thickness of the sash. Cut a dowel ⁵⁄₁₆ inch in diameter, coat it with glue, and tap it into the hole with a hammer. After the glue has set, trim and sand the dowel flush with the stile.

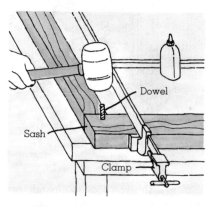

If the sash doesn't permit either of the above treatments, clamp the rails together and screw flat metal reinforcing angles in place. Position the angles so they don't interfere with the movement of the window.

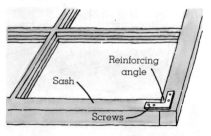

Replacing a broken sash cord or chain

When a sash cord or chain is broken, the sash may not stay open or may jam in a partly open position. Though you'll have to remove the sash from its frame, replacing a cord or chain isn't difficult. While you have the sash out of the frame, it's a good idea to replace both cords and chains, preferably with long-lasting chains or tension-spring or spiral-lift balances.

Removing the old cord. To get to the weights, remove the stop molding and ease out the lower sash; unscrew and pry out the access plates. If a plate has been painted over, tap the area with a hammer until cracks reveal the plate's outline. If your window has no access plates, you'll have to remove the casing to reach the weights.

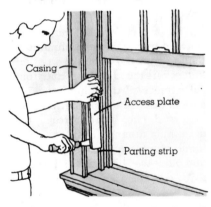

Replacing the cord. To thread the new cord, tie a string weighted by a small screw to one end of the cord, and feed the string over the pulley (see drawing above right). When the string appears at the opening, pull the cord through and tie the cord to the weight.

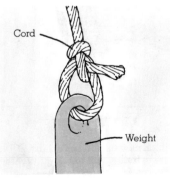

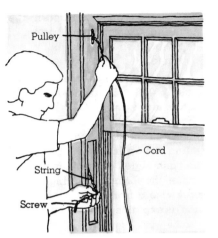

To attach the new cord to the sash, rest the sash on the stool and pull down on the cord until the weight touches the pulley; let the weight drop about 2 inches, and thread the cord into the groove at the side of the sash.

Knot the cord at the level of the knot hole in the sash, clip off the extra length, and insert the knot in the hole. Check the length of the cord by raising the sash to the top of the frame—the weight should hang about 3 inches above the sill. Adjust the cord length, if necessary.

To replace the cord with chain, slide a nail through a link at one end of the chain to keep it from slipping through while you feed the other end over the pulley. Loop the chain through the hole in the weight, securing the free end to the chain with wire (see drawing above right). Before putting the weight back into its pocket, clear the opening of any debris or protruding nails.

To attach the chain to the sash, thread the chain into the sash groove and secure it with wood screws inserted through two of its links into the sash. Adjust the length of the chain in the same way as for a sash cord.

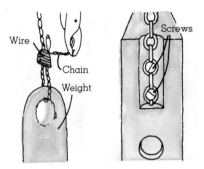

Before replacing the stops and access plates, move the sash up and down in its tracks to see if it operates smoothly. Then screw the access plates back into place. Reseat the stop moldings, using a cardboard shim as a guide to prevent the stops from binding the sash; be sure to nail above and below the access plates, since nails driven into the plates won't hold.

Replacing a tension-spring balance

If any part of a tension-spring balance breaks, you have to remove the unit and install an entirely new one. Many double-hung windows made in the last 30 years use this type of balance instead of weights and pulleys. In this system, a balance unit with a spring-loaded drum inside fits into the frame; a flexible metal tape hooks onto a bracket screwed to the sash.

To replace the unit, remove the stop (see page 87) on the side of the window where the spring balance is broken, and ease the sash out of its channel. Unhook the tape and let it wind back on the drum. Remove the screws from the drum plate and pry the unit out.

Insert the new balance into the jamb pocket and secure it with woodscrews. Pull the tape down with pliers and hook the end to the bracket on the sash. Ease the sash back into its channel, check its operation, and reseat the stop (see page 87).

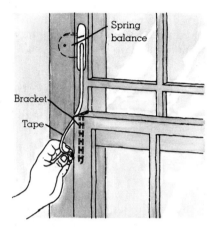

Replacing a spiral-lift balance

Like the tension-spring balance, the spiral-lift balance has to be replaced with a new unit if a part breaks. A recent innovation, the spiral-lift balance consists of a spring-loaded spiral rod encased in a metal or plastic tube; the tube rests in the channel in the side of the stile. Attached to the bottom of the sash, the rod holds the sash in any position. Adjusting the spring tension by rotating the rod assures that the sash is properly balanced.

To remove a broken balance, pry out the stop on the affected side and unscrew the tube where it's fastened to the top of the jamb (see drawing at right). Let the spring unwind; then angle the sash out of the frame. If the rod is attached to the bottom of the sash with a detachable hook, unhook it; support the sash in a raised position with a wooden block, and unscrew and remove the mounting bracket.

To replace the balance, position a new tube in the channel, and screw it into the top of the jamb. Pull the spiral rod down as far as it will go, and turn the rod clockwise about four complete turns to tighten the spring (see drawing at far right). Let the rod retract into the tube far

enough so you can fasten the mounting bracket to the bottom of the sash. Ease the sash back into the frame.

Check the movement of the sash by sliding it up and down. If it moves up when you release it, loosen the spring by detaching the tube from the top of the jamb and letting the spring unwind a bit. If the sash slides down, you need to tighten the spring by turning the rod clockwise a few times. Reseat the stop as explained on page 87.

Restoring a damaged sill

Of all window parts, the sill on the exterior of the house receives the greatest amount of abuse. Unless covered with vinyl or metal sheathing, the sill can deteriorate quickly due to continual contact with water. When the wood is damaged but not completely rotted through, you can restore the sill, making a water-repellent surface that slopes away from the house.

One way to restore a sill and discourage rotting is to apply a generous coating of epoxy resin (the kind used for boat repairs). After the resin dries, you can build up the surface of the sill to the proper slope by applying the epoxy filler used for boat repairs.

Another method of prolonging sill life is to fill cracks in the wood with linseed oil and putty. After cleaning the surface, soak the sill with a pentachlorophenol wood preservative. When the preservative dries (in about 24 hours), pour boiled linseed oil over the sill, and work it into the wood and the cracks with a brush. Repeat the linseed oil application the next day. When the wood is completely dry, fill any cracks or holes with putty. Wait a few days for a skin to form over the putty; then prime and paint the sill.

If you have badly damaged sills that must be built up, apply wood putty or a wood filler made of fine sawdust, and a waterproof glue. For jobs requiring more than a ¼-inch buildup, apply two or more coatings of wood filler; let each coat dry completely before applying the next. Sand, prime, and paint the sill after the last layer of filler has dried.

You can cover a sill that's deteriorated with a piece of aluminum. Using heavy paper, make a pattern that covers the top, sides, and front; cut a piece of aluminum sheet to match. Caulk the joints between the sill and the house, form the aluminum around the sill, and nail it into place. Caulk any open joints and paint the sill to match the trim.

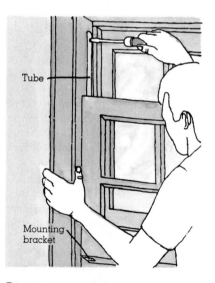

Remove stop on affected side and unscrew tube from frame. Angle sash from frame and remove balance.

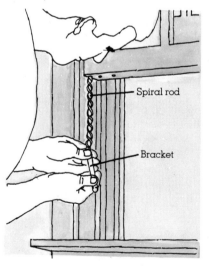

Position new tube in sash channel and screw to frame. Pull rod down, tighten four turns, and attach to sash.

CASEMENT AND AWNING WINDOWS

The operation and care of casement and awning windows, as well as the inverted awnings called hoppers, are similar. In both window types, the sash is hinged at the side, top, or bottom, and is operated by a sliding rod or a crank and gear mechanism.

To keep the hardware working smoothly in casement and awning windows, you'll occasionally need to lubricate it with a few drops of a light household oil or silicone spray. On a casement, apply the lubricant to the hinges, the pivot of the latch, the extension-arm track, and the base of the crank. On an awning window, oil or spray the hinges, the joints between the sash

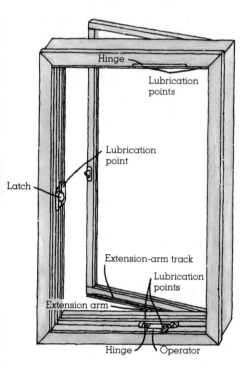

and the scissor arms of the operator, the pivots in the middle of each scissor arm, and the base of the crank.

Except for an occasional cleaning and lubrication of the crank and arm, or the tightening of loose hinges, these windows, especially when made of metal, seldom need repair. But if the gears concealed inside the crank assembly become clogged or worn, you'll need to clean, lubricate, or replace them.

Wood casements or awnings require extra attention. They can shrink, swell, warp, or become jammed with paint.

Easing a binding sash

If paint is preventing the sash from closing, scrape away any excess paint, and sand the surface smooth. If the sash is swollen, sand, with coarse sandpaper the part that rubs against the stop; then smooth it with fine sandpaper or plane it lightly. If you expose bare wood, coat it with sealer to prevent future swelling, and repaint it. If the stop has swollen, remove, sand, and reseat it (see page 87).

If the sash doesn't close because of loose hinges, see directions at right to adjust them.

Fixing a warped sash

You can compensate for a mild warp in a wood sash by adjusting the stop molding (see page 87) or by counter-warping; for flat metal sashes, try the counter-warping method, but be careful that you don't break the glass.

To counter-warp a sash, close the sash until some part touches the frame. Set a small wood block about ⅜ inch thick at this point to force the sash away from the frame.

At the same time, force the lagging corner of the sash tightly closed and secure it as shown in the drawing above. Leave the sash in this position for a week. The stress in the opposite direction should leave the sash almost completely warp-free.

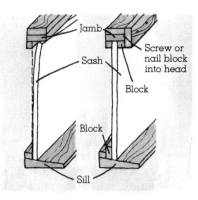

Adjusting hinges

If a sash sags or sticks in its frame, its hinges probably need adjusting or replacing. If a hinge pin is loose in its guides, you'll have to replace the entire hinge with an identical model. But if the screws have worked loose or the hinge is recessed too deeply in the jamb, tightening and shimming should solve the problem.

While working on the hinges, support the sash on the latch side with a wedge driven between the sash and the frame.

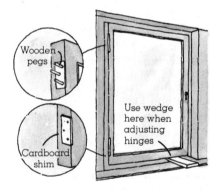

Tightening screws. If the screws that fasten the hinge leaf to the jamb cannot be tightened, the screw holes may have become enlarged. To repair, cut wooden pegs or dowels to size, coat them with glue, and drive them into the holes (see drawing above). After the glue dries, use a chisel to trim the pegs flush; then drill pilot holes into them and replace the hinges.

Shimming hinges. A hinge recessed too deeply in the jam or sash causes the sash to bind at the diagonally opposite end on the latch side.

A simple cure is to shim the hinge (see drawing on previous page). Supporting the open sash with a wedge inserted between the sash and the sill on the latch side, free the hinge pin by hammering from below on a nail or punch. Remove the hinge leaf on the jamb side. Using the hinge leaf as a template, cut a shim, complete with screw holes, from noncompressible cardboard (the type used for file folders). Make the shim slightly smaller in all dimensions. Place the shim between the hinge leaf and the jamb, and fasten the hinge with screws. If the sash is still binding, use an additional shim.

Repairing the window operators

The movement of older casement and awning windows is usually controlled by a sliding rod; the more recent versions use a crank and gear mechanism to control their operation.

If a casement or awning sash resists opening and closing, look for hardened grease or paint on the sliding rod or in the tracks and gears of the crank. Cleaning and lubricating the channel and the crank and gear assembly usually solves the problem. If the gears are worn, you'll probably have to replace the entire unit.

To ease the movement of a rod that slides through a fixed mount, remove any paint or dirt with steel wool and lubricate the rod lightly with paraffin. Make sure the pivot points are lubricated and the screws holding the mounts to the sash and the stool are fastened securely.

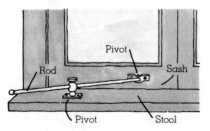

If the rod assembly uses a shoe that slides in a stool-mounted channel, check the channel for debris or layered paint. Unscrew the channel from the sill, clean both the channel and the stool, and lubricate with paraffin before replacing the channel. Tighten the screws on the pivot mount fastened to the sash and oil the pivot points on both the stool and the sash.

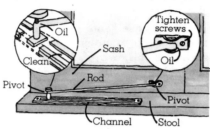

To clean the extension-arm track in a casement that operates with a crank, open the window fully and scrape out any caked grease, dirt, or paint with a wire brush. Take care to clean out the lip of the track, as well. Lubricate the inside of the track lightly with petroleum jelly or silicone spray; remove any excess lubricant. Open and close the window several times.

To check the gear assembly, you'll have to unfasten and remove the operator. Open the window partially and remove the screws that fasten the operator to the frame. To disengage the extension arm from its track on a casement, slide the arm along until it slips free. On an awning window, release the arms from the mounting bracket fastened to the bottom of the sash. Then pull the operator indoors through the window frame.

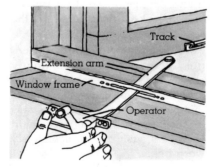

Inspect the gears carefully. If the teeth are damaged or worn, replace the unit with a new one. If you have a casement window, be sure the new unit cranks in the same direction as the old one.

If the gear teeth are sharp, but clogged with dirt or grease, remove the dirt with a piece of coat-hanger wire, or clean the assembly with a solvent, such as kerosene, and let it dry. Lubricate the metal gears with a graphite powder, silicone, or petroleum jelly; then turn the crank several times to spread the lubricant. Use silicone spray on nylon gears; if they still malfunction, replace the entire assembly.

SLIDING WINDOWS

Sliding window sashes move along metal or vinyl tracks fitted into the window frame at the top and bottom. To ease their movement, larger sashes often have plastic rollers attached at the top and bottom or at the bottom alone.

A dirty or bent track, or paint sealing the sash to the frame can cause a sliding sash to stick or bind. The window can jam or not close properly if catches bend or become loose or damaged.

To free a paint-clogged sash, score the paint with a sharp utility knife and rock the sash vertically. If you're faced with track and catch problems, you'll have to remove the sash from the frame first. Just lift the sash up and out, or align the top rollers with key notches and then remove the sash.

Fixing track problems

To clean and lubricate the track, you'll need a wire brush, a screwdriver, and some paraffin or paste wax. Clean out any dirt with the brush; for stubborn particles, use the blade of the screwdriver. Lubricate the track with paraffin.

To straighten a bent track, slide a block of wood into the channel where the metal is bent. With a hammer, tap the block against the

(Continued on page 94)

Cold air entering your house in winter accounts for up to 35 percent of your heating load. Weatherstripping your windows can help reduce that load by 20 percent.

Most windows manufactured in recent years were weatherstripped at the factory. Many older windows were not, but most of these can be sealed with one of the ordinary types of weatherstripping sold in building supply stores.

Selection and installation tips

The types of weatherstripping most commonly used are spring metal or plastic, pliable gasket, and compressible felt. Base your choice on window type, appearance, and budget.

Discussed here for wood double-hung and casement and other hinged windows are the kinds of weatherstripping available and the installation method for each. For more information, as well as weatherstripping instructions for other types of windows, see the Sunset book *Insulation & Weatherstripping.*

Double-hung windows.
Spring-metal or plastic weatherstripping works best for these windows. Though slightly more difficult to install than pliable gasket, it's more durable and less visible.

Spring-type weatherstripping made from bronze is bent in the shape of a V or slightly angled; made from plastic, it's shaped like a

V. Each type fastens with brads to the window frame, except at the bottom, where it's often nailed to the bottom of the sash rather than to the stool. For correct positioning, see the illustration below.

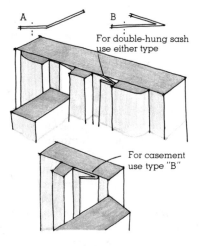

A.

B.

For double-hung sash use either type

For casement use type "B"

Casement windows.
Pliable gasket weatherstripping or compressible felt strips work well with casement and other hinged windows. Some metal types can be weatherstripped with a spring-metal strip, available on special order, that slips over the edges of the sash.

Pliable-gasket weatherstripping varieties include metal-edged tubular vinyl and foam, and sponge. These are adhesive-backed or attach with brads to the window stops so the sash presses lightly against them. Though not visible from the inside, the strips may be very visible from the outside.

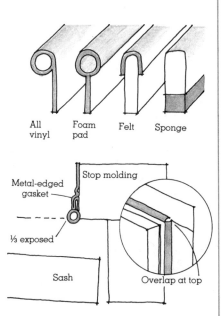

All vinyl   Foam pad   Felt   Sponge

Metal-edged gasket

Stop molding

⅓ exposed

Sash

Overlap at top

Compressible felt strips are attached to a metal casement where the sash meets the stop and frame, as shown. Some strips are fastened with nails or glue; others are adhesive-backed. Though the strips wear out quickly, they're good for a warped window that doesn't close tightly.

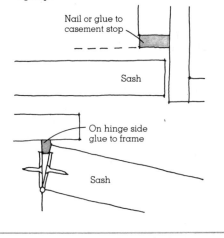

Nail or glue to casement stop

Sash

On hinge side glue to frame

Sash

. . . *Continued from page 92*

metal, working from the sides of the bent spot toward the middle.

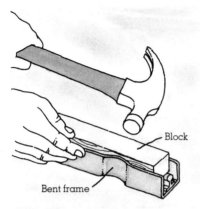

Bent frame

Block

If the rollers stick, lubricate them lightly with graphite powder or silicone lubricant until they move freely. If the rollers are broken, you'll have to take the sash to a glazier to have them replaced.

Fixing catches

Most sliding windows have some variation of a hook-and-eye catch; others use a catch-plate and a spring-loaded dog.

The hook-and-eye consists of a hook-shaped lever that pivots on a point and fastens to some part of the window frame. If the lever malfunctions, replacement is the easiest course; most levers screw into place.

The catch-plate and dog latch malfunctions either because the catch-plate under the rail gets bent from wear so the dog can't strike it properly, or because the dog gets loose from its position in the bottom of the sash.

To repair a bent catch-plate, first note how much it will have to be reshaped to bring it flush with the widest diameter of the rail; then unscrew it from its position alongside the rail. Clamp the catch-plate in a vise; using pliers or a hammer, bend it to the needed angle. Replace and check the operation of the latch—it should click as the window closes and should have to be depressed fully for the window to open.

To secure a loose dog, remove the sash from the frame; then unscrew the dog from the bottom of the sash. Lay the sash flat on a stable surface, replace the dog in its proper position, and secure it.

To replace a worn or broken dog, unscrew the dog from the sash, buy a replacement part, and install the new dog.

REPLACING BROKEN PANES

Chances are that at some time you'll have a cracked or shattered pane in a window in your house. But don't let it shatter your nerves; replacing a pane, especially one smaller than 2 by 3 feet, is easier than you might imagine. Larger panes, though, are best left to a professional.

When working with glass, observe these simple safety rules: wear heavy gloves when removing broken glass or handling loose panes; wear goggles when prying out shards or cutting glass; pad glass with several layers of newspaper or padded material when transporting it; and dispose of glass slivers immediately after cleaning a sash or cutting glass.

You can buy glass cut to size; but if you're replacing more than one pane, you may want to cut the glass yourself.

To determine the size pane you need, measure the opening in the sash at its widest points *after* removing all broken glass and old putty, and subtract ⅛ inch from each dimension. When working with old wood sashes, be sure to measure at several points to allow for the sash being out of square.

To remove broken glass, tape newspaper to the inside of the sash to catch any fragments. Working from the outside, wiggle the shards back and forth to free them from the putty. Working from the top of the sash, remove bits of glass and old putty with a chisel. If the putty is hard, soak it in linseed oil for half

an hour, or soften it by heating it gently with a propane torch or a soldering iron; chisel the softened putty off the sash.

Use pliers to extract glazier's points from the sash; remove the clips in a metal sash by pinching them together and pulling them from their holes in the sash.

Reglazing wood sashes

Removing broken glass and setting new glass in a wood sash is relatively easy (see drawings on opposite page). You may need a little practice to bevel the putty; if you have trouble, remove it and try again.

Reglazing metal sashes

In some metal sashes, the glass is held in place with clips and putty; in others, rubber seals, rubber gaskets, or metal or plastic moldings secure the glass.

Clips and putty. To replace a pane in a puttied sash, clean and prepare the sash as explained above and shown on the next page. Lay a thin bead of putty in the channel, and press the new pane of glass into the putty. To secure the glass, push clips into the holes in the sash; apply putty around the pane and smooth it into a bevel.

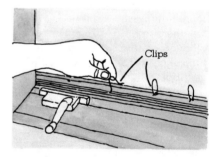

Clips

Rubber seals. If the glass is sandwiched between two halves of the sash—usually two nearly flat pieces of metal screwed together at the corners—replace the glass from the inside.

Unscrew the sash halves and remove the inside piece. In this kind of sash, the rubber seals are usually attached to the sash, so you only

REGLAZING A WOOD SASH

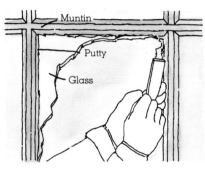

Chisel bits of glass and old putty out of sash. Propane torch will soften hard putty. Coat wood with linseed oil or sealer so putty oils are not drawn out, causing putty to become brittle.

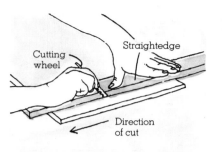

If glass isn't precut, measure opening and cut glass ⅛ inch smaller in each dimension. Dip cutting wheel in kerosene and score glass deeply with glass cutter.

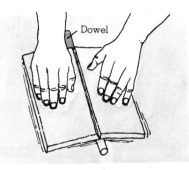

To break glass, place score over small dowel and press down on both sides, or tap along underside of score with ball end of cutter. If break is uneven, nibble off pieces using notches on cutter.

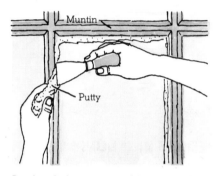

Lay bead of putty around frame so putty fills recess in which glass rests. Make bead ⅛ to ¼ inch thick to help correct irregularities in frame and cushion glass.

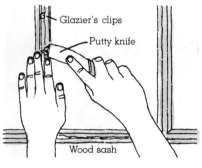

Press glass pane into putty bead and secure with glazier's clips. Press clips into frame with a putty knife; use two clips to a side for small panes and one every 6 inches for larger ones.

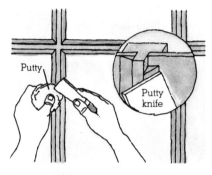

Apply sealing bead of putty. Bead should be flush with outer edge of frame and should come as high as inner edge (inside of glass). Press firmly for good seal and trim excess as you work.

have to brush out any glass fragments, set a new pane against one sash half, replace the other half of the sash, and secure it with screws.

Rubber gaskets. In this type of sash, the glass sits on one continuous removable rubber gasket (or four separate ones); the gasket is fitted into molded channels of a sash screwed together at the corners. To replace the glass, remove the screws from a vertical end of the sash and pull the end away from the rest of the sash. Clean the old glass from the gasket, and pull the gasket around the new pane, slide the pane into the sash, and resecure the end.

Metal or plastic moldings. To replace glass in a sash with snap-out moldings, remove any broken glass and loosen one end of a piece of molding from the sash by insert-ing the tip of a putty knife where two ends meet. Pull out the loosened strip; remove remaining strips in the same manner. Clean the frame and position the new pane. Replace the moldings, starting with the short pieces, by pushing each piece into place with your hands. If the moldings look even slightly damaged, replace them.

PAINTING FOR PRESERVATION

An unpainted wood sash can rot and crack from exposure to moisture and the drying effects of the sun; an unpainted steel sash, unless treated, can rust and corrode.

To prolong the life of your windows and keep them looking attractive, paint the sashes at the first sign of deterioration.

To prepare a wood sash for painting, remove all loose paint and sand the surface smooth. Applying a wood preservative before painting serves two purposes: it waterproofs the sash and acts as a primer. Let it dry overnight.

Clean and prepare a painted steel sash the same way you prepare a wood sash, making sure that sanding removes all traces of rust and corrosion. You don't need to apply a wood preservative. Prime the window and let it dry thoroughly before painting.

To protect glass from paint smears, you may want to place masking tape around its edges. The paint should extend 1/16 inch onto the glass for a weather seal. An angled sash brush may be all you'll need to keep paint off the glass; it's especially useful when you're painting muntins.

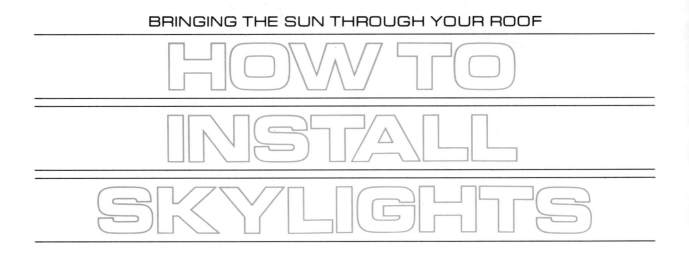

HOW TO INSTALL SKYLIGHTS

Choosing the right kind of skylight is the first step in bringing sunshine, moonbeams, and starlight into your home. Next come the challenges of cutting a hole in your roof, framing it, and sealing it against wind, rain, and snow.

If you're considering installing a skylight yourself, be sure to read the following pages very carefully to learn what's involved. Penetrating roofing materials and framing the opening below can be difficult and demanding, even for experts. Once you understand the processes and the pitfalls of installing a skylight, you'll be able to decide whether this is work for you or a professional.

Most skylights consist of a preframed plastic window that you buy and attach to the roof surface. Sometimes, a shutter or light diffuser for light control at ceiling level is included.

If your roof is flat or moderately sloped (up to 6 in 12, which means it rises vertically no more than 6 feet for every 12 horizontal feet) and covered with asphalt or wood shingles, installing an off-the-shelf skylight should present no major problems, as long as you work carefully. Be sure to check page 20 for the proper choice of a curb-mounted or a self-flashing skylight. For more information on working on a roof, see the roof safety feature on page 103, and the *Sunset* book *Do-It-Yourself Roofing & Siding*.

Even the most skilled do-it-yourselfer may require professional help under certain conditions. You'd be wise to have a contractor install a skylight larger than 48 inches square; also rely on professional installation if your roof has a slope greater than 6 in 12 or is surfaced with slippery tiles or slate.

If you have a built-up roof covered with polyurethane foam or roofing felt and hot-mopped asphalt, you may be able to install the skylight yourself, but you might prefer to hire a contractor to rebuild the roofing around the skylight. (See page 22 for information on working with professionals.)

Since work of this type is governed by local codes, check your plans with the building department. You may need a building permit.

TOOLS AND SUPPLIES

Safety equipment and a sturdy ladder are essentials (see page 103). The other tools and supplies you'll need to install a skylight vary, depending on your roof and your skylight's design. Also check the manufacturer's installation instructions for any additional tools and supplies required.

Tools of the trade

You probably already have most of the tools required. Commonly used tools include these:

- 12-foot steel tape measure to take vertical and horizontal measurements and to lay out openings;
- 16 to 20-ounce claw hammer with a flat mesh face to frame the opening;
- 14 to 16-ounce claw hammer with a convex head to nail wallboard to a light shaft, and to frame the opening if you don't have the hammer described above;
- level, at least 24 inches long, to level and plumb structural members and to lay out the openings;

- plumb bob to locate one point vertically above another point;

- chalk line to outline roof and ceiling openings;

- wood chisel to cut out pieces of roofing material and sheathing boards;

- shingle nail puller or crowbar to remove shingles, roofing felt, and sheathing boards;

- combination or framing square to mark straight or angled cuts;

- sliding T-bevel to measure angles in a light shaft;

- flashlight or extension light to explore attic or crawl space;

- hand drill or ¼ or ⅜-inch electric drill (with twist bit) to drill holes to locate the corners of the ceiling and roof openings;

- tin snips to trim asphalt shingles and sheet-metal flashing;

- nailsets to drive in nails—a ³⁄₁₆-inch and a ³⁄₃₂-inch nailset will meet most of your needs;

- handsaw or 7¼-inch circular saw with all-purpose blade to cut through roof;

- keyhole or reciprocating saw to cut through the ceiling or to cut wood in tight spots;

- caulking gun to shoot caulking compound underneath flashing and to apply sealants;

- utility knife to score wallboard;

- goggles and painter's mask to protect eyes and nose.

Supplies and installation tips

Both the design of your skylight and the type of roof on your house dictate the materials you'll need for installing your skylight. Check local building codes for specific requirements.

Lumber. You'll need the same size lumber for framing roof and ceiling openings as that used for rafters and joists in your home (usually 2 by 6 or 2 by 4). To build a skylight curb, the frame that holds a curb-mounted skylight above the roof, you'll probably use 2 by 6 lumber. But if you're installing a skylight in an open-beam ceiling (see page 109), you'll have to use 2 by 8, 2 by 10, or wider lumber.

To frame the light shaft, the passage through which light from the roof enters the room, you'll need a 2 by 4 stud every 16 inches and two at each corner, unless your building code directs differently.

Wallboard or plywood. Either wallboard or plywood can be used

TOOLS OF THE TRADE

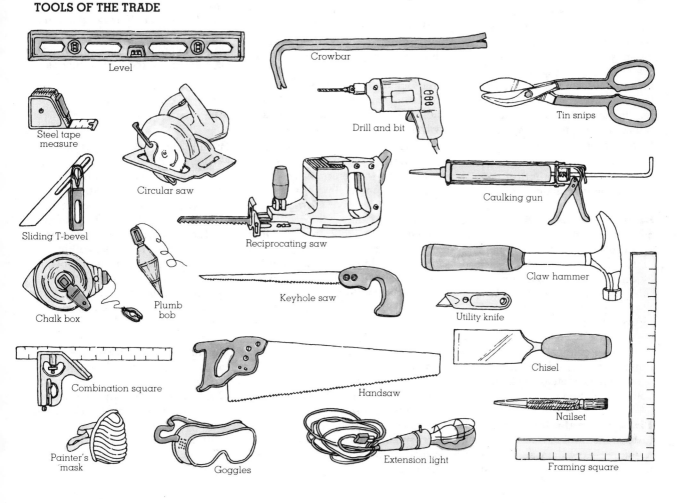

Level

Crowbar

Drill and bit

Tin snips

Steel tape measure

Circular saw

Caulking gun

Sliding T-bevel

Reciprocating saw

Claw hammer

Chalk box

Plumb bob

Keyhole saw

Utility knife

Chisel

Combination square

Handsaw

Nailset

Painter's mask

Goggles

Extension light

Framing square

to finish the light shaft. If you're planning to use the plywood, check your local building code; you may be required to use a fire-resistant wallboard.

Metal flashing. If you're not installing a self-flashing skylight, you'll need metal flashing to seal the roof opening against leaks. Because it's difficult to seal flashing joints without soldering, you may want to have a sheet-metal shop make the flashing unless you have a propane torch or large soldering iron.

To order flashing, you'll need to know the outside dimensions and height of the curb, the slope of the roof, and the type of roofing material. Tell the sheet-metal shop that you want the saddle part of the flashing (see page 102) to extend two shingles beyond the curb.

Nails. Generally, you can use 16-penny common nails to frame the roof opening and to build the curb (on a shake roof, though, use 20-penny to mark the opening), 6 or 8-penny common nails for bracing the curb, 1½-inch galvanized roofing nails for securing the flashing to the curb, wallboard nails for finishing the light shaft, and 1½ to 2-inch finishing nails for nailing molding to the ceiling opening.

To secure the curb to the roof in open-beam construction, you'll need 8-penny finishing nails.

Sealing compounds. Roofing cement, a waterproofing agent, is available in caulking tubes (for shake or shingle roofs) or 1 and 5-gallon cans (for built-up roofs). Silicone sealant applied between the skylight and the curb works best for sealing the unit to the top of the curb. Caulking compound is used to seal the flashing. Check with a building supply dealer for the type of sealing compound you'll need for your installation.

Finishing materials. If you want to trim the ceiling opening, you'll need molding, finishing nails, nailset, and wood putty. Installing lights in the shaft (see page 111) requires fixtures and wiring materials.

PREPARING THE OPENINGS

Installing a skylight in a room that has a finished ceiling with an attic or crawl space above it involves planning both a ceiling opening and a roof opening. On the other hand, you'll need to lay out only one opening if the area you're working in has an open-beam ceiling. Instructions for installing a skylight in an open-beam ceiling begin on page 109.

Regardless of the type of construction, the size of the roof opening will be determined by the size of the skylight you're installing. Generally, the dimensions of the roof opening in a house with finished ceilings are the same as the inside dimensions of the skylight or of the curb if it's a curb-mounted unit.

Most manufacturers provide the necessary dimensions along with installation instructions. If a manufacturer gives the curb's *outside* dimensions, deduct twice the curb's thickness from the length and width to determine the size of the opening.

Contractors differ on the methods they use to determine the location of roof and ceiling openings in homes with attics or crawl spaces. Some contractors cut the opening in the ceiling before cutting the roof opening. Others cut the roof opening first, and this is the method described below; it allows you to adjust to the conditions in your home.

Planning and marking the ceiling opening

Whether your desire is for moonbeams on your bed, diffused light for your art projects, or sunlight splashing across your dining room table, the location of your ceiling opening depends on where you want the light and what kind of light you need (see page 17).

Even after you've identified the ideal location, you may want to make some adjustments if you discover some structural impediment when you explore your attic.

The size of the ceiling opening depends not only on the skylight's size, but also on the amount of light you want to bring in. The light enters the room through a light shaft, which can be straight, angled, or splayed (see page 101).

An angled or splayed light shaft allows you to offset the roof opening from the ceiling opening. If you want to maximize the amount of light coming into the room, make the ceiling opening larger than the roof opening and connect them with a splayed light shaft; you can splay any or all shaft walls.

After you've decided on the location and size of the ceiling opening, mark the four corners and the center of the proposed opening. Drive nails deeply enough through these five points so you can find them in the attic. If any of the nails hits solid wood, you may want to move the proposed opening or adjust its size to avoid the obstruction.

Planning and marking the roof opening

Much of the work of installing the skylight is done from the attic or crawl space. If you don't have convenient access to your attic or your attic is not roomy enough to work in, you'll need to cut a hole big enough to climb through or work through (from ladder or platform) within the proposed opening, at one side of the center. Then, after you've marked the center of the roof opening, you can cut the ceiling opening for access (see page 105).

Gathering materials. Assemble the tools and materials you'll need for laying out the roof opening: plumb bob, steel tape measure, straightedge, square, drill and bit (slightly smaller than a 16-penny common nail), some 16-penny nails (20-penny if you have a heavy shake roof), and a pencil.

SKYLIGHT FRAMING

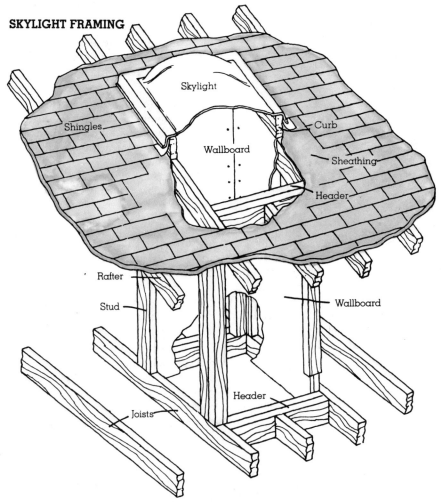

- Skylight
- Shingles
- Wallboard
- Curb
- Sheathing
- Header
- Rafter
- Stud
- Wallboard
- Header
- Joists

You'll need some light, too. Though you can get by a with a flashlight if there's no attic light fixture, you may want to rig a clamp-on extension light. Unless your attic has a floor, you'll also need boards or plywood panels to lay over the joists so you can safely maneuver without falling through the ceiling.

If your attic is insulated, wear clothing that will protect you against insulation material: gloves, a long-sleeved shirt, long pants, a painter's mask, and goggles.

Checking for obstructions. Clear away any insulation material covering the area of your proposed ceiling opening. Locate the five nails that were driven through from the ceiling below. Look for obstructions—wires, pipes, or heating or cooling ducts—within the area of the proposed opening. If you find any and don't want to move or adjust the size of the opening, you'll

have to move the obstruction (see page 70).

To save yourself work when you're framing the ceiling opening, try to arrange the opening so two opposite sides butt up against the facing sides of two joists.

Measuring the opening. To locate the center of the roof opening, hang a plumb bob from the underside of the roof with the point of the bob over the center nail in the ceil-

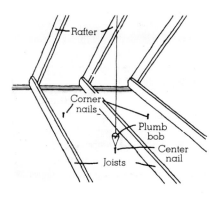

- Rafter
- Corner nails
- Plumb bob
- Center nail
- Joists

ing opening. Mark this point clearly on the underside of the roof.

With your tape, square, and straightedge, mark the manufacturer's recommended dimensions for the roof opening on the underside of the roof.

You can simplify the framing of the opening by locating at least one edge (preferably two) against a rafter.

Check the area of the roof opening for obstructions. If you find wires, pipes, or heating or cooling ducts, you can either move the opening or move the obstruction (see page 70). If the roof ridge or a purlin (a structural member positioned at right angles to the rafters) crosses the opening, you'll have to relocate the opening and use an angled or splayed light shaft between the roof and the ceiling.

Marking the corners. You'll want to be able to find the corners of the opening when you go up on the roof. Drill a hole at each corner and drive a 16-penny nail (20-penny for a shake roof) through each hole.

- Sheathing
- Rafter
- Drill
- Roof opening marks

OPENING THE ROOF

The thought of cutting a hole in your roof needn't conjure up images of dripping water destroying your living room carpet, as long as you know how to seal that opening against the vagaries of nature. And speaking of nature, do the roof work on a day with zero rain probability, and plan on having the skylight installed by the end of the day. Even then, you'd be wise to have a tarp handy, just in case.

(Continued on next page)

. . . *Continued from page 99*

The following pages describe how to build the skylight curb, if needed, and how to cut and frame the opening. Variations for different types of roofing—shingle, shake, and asphalt—are also discussed.

Walk very carefully when you're on the roof—the fewer shakes or shingles you disturb, the better. But put your own safety first. If your roof is moderately sloping, secure a footplank or ladder. For additional tips on working safely on a roof, see the special feature on page 103 and the *Sunset* book *Do-It-Yourself Roofing & Siding*.

Building a curb

Before you can begin cutting through the roof, you'll have to build a curb, or box frame, for your skylight if it's the curb-mounted type. You may find it convenient to assemble the curb on the roof. If your skylight boasts an integral curb, or is self-flashing and sits directly on the sheathing, you can avoid this step.

The curb should raise the skylight at least 4 inches above the roofing material. Usually 2 by 6 lumber works well for shingle, shake, and built-up roofs.

The *inside* dimensions of the curb should equal the dimensions specified by the manufacturer for the roof opening. Mark the lumber for cuts, taking care to keep knots away from the ends. Cut the pieces. As a further precaution against split ends, drill pilot holes for nails; then nail the pieces together.

Check the curb for squareness by measuring diagonally from corner to corner; the distances should be identical. You can also use a framing square.

It's a good idea to brace two opposite corners of the curb to keep it square until you're ready to nail it in place. Make the braces from lengths of wood or cut triangles from ½-inch plywood. Nail in the braces with 6 or 8-penny common nails; drive the nails halfway down so you can remove them easily later on.

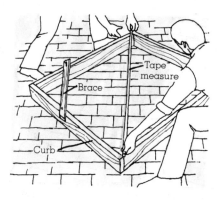

Marking the roof

In a home with finished ceilings, you mark the roof opening and the roofing material that needs to be removed in exactly the same manner for either a sloped or a flat roof. The amount of roofing material you remove to allow for the flashing and water runoff varies, depending on the type of roofing and the kind of skylight you use. To mark the roof if you have open-beam construction, see page 109.

For a curb-mounted skylight, set the curb over the four nails protruding through the roof. If the curb is the right size, there'll be a nail in each inside corner.

For a wood or asphalt shingle roof, use chalk, pencil, or a utility knife to mark lines on the roof along the outside edges of the sides of the curb. Extend the lines you just outlined 3 inches beyond the top and bottom corners of the curb. Mark a line between these points and parallel to the top and bottom of the curb. This is the area from which you'll remove the roofing material (see below).

If you have a heavy shake roof, mark lines on the roof ½ inch away from the outside edges of the sides of the curb; extend those lines 3 inches to the top and bottom, and connect them in the manner described above.

After you've marked the lines, you can set the curb aside.

For a self-flashing skylight, make your measurements from the sides of the proposed roof opening

marked by the four nails. Mark lines appoximately 10 inches beyond the nails on the top and the two sides, and 2 inches below the nails on the bottom.

On a flat roof (hot-mopped asphalt or foam), mark lines 10 inches beyond the nails on all four sides. You'll have to remove the gravel first.

Cutting through roofing materials

Though you can use hand tools to cut through a roof, a circular saw is easier and faster. A combination blade is best for cutting through wood shingles or shakes. You may find that a utility knife works better than a circular saw to cut through asphalt shingles.

Use safety precautions when working with any power tool: make sure the equipment is properly grounded, wear goggles or safety glasses, avoid awkward positions, and keep out of the line of the blade. Be alert while sawing—a blade that binds can throw you off the roof.

To cut through shingles or shakes for a curb-mounted skylight or through built-up roofing for a self-flashing skylight, adjust the depth of cut on your saw so the blade cuts through the roofing material, but not through the wood sheathing underneath. Resting the front of the saw's sole plate on the roof, align the saw blade with the chalk or pencil mark or the knife cut.

Turn on the power and lower the saw until the sole is resting on the roof. Saw slowly and steadily along the marked line until you reach a corner. Repeat for the other sides.

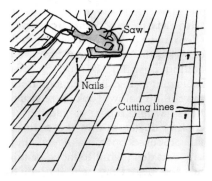

FRAMING FOR OPENINGS

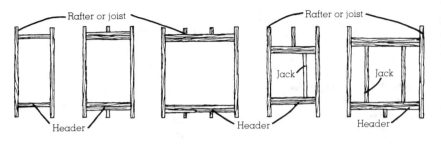

After you've cut around the opening, pry the roofing materials loose with a crowbar and hammer; save asphalt shingles to use for patching around the skylight. Peel off the roofing felt to expose the sheathing.

Determining framing requirements. To determine the framing needed for the opening (see drawing above), carefully examine the structure of the roof around your skylight opening. If your skylight fits exactly between two rafters, you'll need single headers, framing members running perpendicular to the rafters that support the sheathing. If it fits exactly between the rafters on either side of an opening spanning one or more rafters, you'll need double headers to support the sheathing and the cut rafters.

Skylights smaller than the space between the rafters require an opening framed with both headers and jack rafters, framing members running parallel to the rafters between the headers: one jack rafter if the opening abuts one rafter, two if it does not. Lumber used for headers and jack rafters should be the same size as the rafters.

Cutting the sheathing. Stretch the chalk line around the nails that were pushed through the roof, and snap the line between each pair of nails to mark the finished roof opening.

Mark another set of lines in the sheathing around these and parallel to them, depending on your framing requirements (see above):

mark a line at right angles to the rafters at both ends of the finished opening—1½ inches away for a single header, and 3 inches away for a double one if you're using 1½-inch-thick lumber. If you'll be installing jack rafters, mark lines parallel to the rafters 1½ inches away from both sides of the finished opening.

Pull out any nails within 4 inches of the edges of the proposed opening. This avoids damaging the blades of your saw.

With a combination blade in your saw, set the depth of cut just to cut through the sheathing. Cut along the larger outline on the sheathing as described above.

Cutting the rafters

Though rafters crossing the roof opening can be left in place, you may want to remove them for an unobstructed view of the sky. You'll then have to install double headers.

To remove a rafter, use a combination square to mark lines on the rafter to be cut and the rafters on both sides of the opening at a right angle to the cut edge of the roof

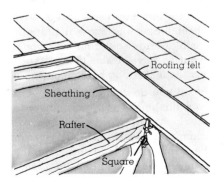

sheathing; if the light shaft will be splayed or angled, mark the lines at the desired angle (see drawings at right). The lines on the rafters on the sides of the opening indicate the placement of the headers.

Before cutting the rafter, support it on each side of the opening with 2 by 4s nailed to the rafter and the ceiling joist below. Leave these supports in place until you've installed the headers.

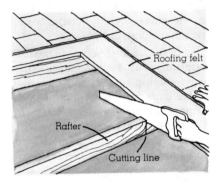

The angle at which you secure the headers to the rafters depends on the angle of the light shaft you're building (see the illustrations below).

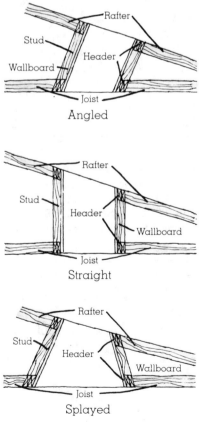

Angled

Straight

Splayed

Framing the roof opening

Whether or not you've cut through any rafters, you'll need to frame the roof opening with headers and possibly jack rafters so the sheathing is supported on all four sides.

Installing double headers. After you've marked the angles of the headers, measure the distance between the rafters. Using lumber that's the same thickness and width as the rafters, cut four pieces to the length measured.

To secure the headers to the rafters, nail double joist hangers to the rafters using special hanger nails; make sure that the bottom of each hanger is aligned with the bottom of the rafter, and the outer side of the U-shaped support is aligned with the line marking the header position.

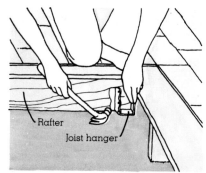

Rafter

Joist hanger

If the header is not perpendicular to the top of the rafter, you may have to cut away any part of the hanger that protrudes above the header. Or you can use framing anchors instead of joist hangers.

Place a header into each facing pair of hangers and nail it to the cut end of the rafter with 16-penny common nails. Put a second header

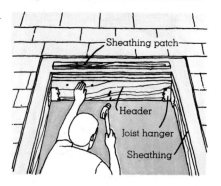

Sheathing patch

Header

Joist hanger

Sheathing

into each pair of hangers and nail it to the first header with 8-penny nails; space the nails 6 inches apart and stagger them along the length of the piece. Nail the joist hanger flanges to the headers. Repeat on the opposite side of the opening.

Installing a single header. Follow the same procedure for measuring as described for double headers (see above); cut two, rather than four, pieces.

Installation is similar to that for a double header; you use only one header for each pair of single-size hangers.

Finishing the framing. If your roof opening doesn't fit exactly between rafters you'll need to install jack rafters between the headers parallel to the rafters (see drawing on page 101). Cut lumber the same size as the rafters to fit between the two headers. Install and nail these pieces in joist hangers nailed to the headers. Cut some plywood the same thickness as the sheathing you removed so it fits on top of the headers and jack rafters, if used. Nail it to the headers with 8-penny common nails.

INSTALLING AND FLASHING THE CURB

If you're installing a self-flashing skylight, you're now ready to position the skylight (see page 104). But if your skylight is a curb-mounted unit, you need to flash the curb. This is the most critical part of the skylight installation—a bad flashing job can result in a leaky roof.

Unless you've worked with sheet metal and have a propane torch or large soldering iron, you'll want to have a sheet metal shop make the flashing pieces for you.

If you do decide to make your own flashings, use lead, easier to work with than copper or aluminum. With little effort, you can bend and solder lead and solder the joints between flashings for a long-

lasting, watertight seal. Make paper patterns of the flashings to fit the curb; form the pieces, and then solder the joints in the saddle and apron flashings.

Flashing a curb so it forms a watertight seal beween the outside and inside of your home requires special care and thoroughness. If you follow the instructions below, and any guidelines from the manufacturer of the skylight, you should be able to enjoy the raindrops dancing on your skylight, instead of dripping into your house.

Saddle flashing. Slide the saddle, or top flashing, underneath both the shingles or shakes and the roofing felt. Remove any nails that keep you from sliding the saddle all the way up under the shingles. As you position the saddle, take care not to puncture the roofing felt, as this can cause leaks.

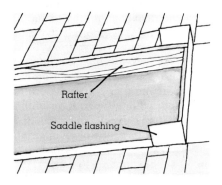

Rafter

Saddle flashing

Set the curb over the roof opening, sliding it up from the bottom until it's perfectly aligned with the opening. Check the curb for squareness. Then, using 16-penny nails, toenail the curb through the sheathing to the frame (rafters and headers). Remove the corner braces from the curb.

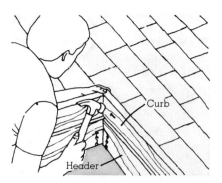

Curb

Header

(Continued on page 104)

If you're installing a skylight, you'll eventually have to get up on the roof. Before you embark on a trip up your ladder, it's important that you know and observe the following safety precautions.

General considerations

Keep these tips in mind every time you approach the roof.

● Wear loose, comfortable clothing, rubber-soled shoes with good ankle support, and a hat for sun protection.

● Work on the roof only in dry, calm, warm weather. A ladder or roof that's wet from rain, frost, or dew can be treacherously slick, and a sudden wind can knock you off balance. Keep grass cuttings and mud off your shoes, as well. Never get on the roof when lightning threatens.

● Once on the roof, be alert for slippery, brittle, or old roofing materials, and rotten decking you could put a foot through.

● Avoid contact both with power lines connected to the house and with television antennas.

● To avoid straining your back, lift only lightweight loads and let your leg muscles do the work.

● Pace yourself and take frequent rests.

● Keep children and pets off the roof and away from the work area; they can be hurt by falling materials.

Safety equipment

The standard safety devices illustrated are available from tool rental companies.

● Metal ladder brackets allow you to hook a ladder over the ridge of a house.

● Toe board jacks nailed to the roof support you and your materials with a 2 by 6 plank. (Use strong, straight-grained lumber no longer than 10 feet unless you support the middle with another jack.) The jacks have notches in them so they can be slipped off the nails. Secure jacks with nails long enough to penetrate sheathing and rafters.

● An angled seat board allows you to sit on a level surface while working. Angles on the sides of the board must match the slope of your roof.

● Scaffolding, useful if you're installing a large skylight, can be rented from tool supply companies.

Ladders

Inspect your ladder for cracks or weaknesses in the rungs before you lean it against the house. The ladder should be long enough so that at least two rungs extend above the eaves. Place the base of the ladder on firm, level ground at a measured distance from the side of the house—that distance should equal a quarter of the vertical distance from the ground to the top rung.

Get on and off by stepping onto the center of the rung; use both hands.

If the ladder is to stand on a slick surface, install rubber safety shoes (they're available at home improvement centers).

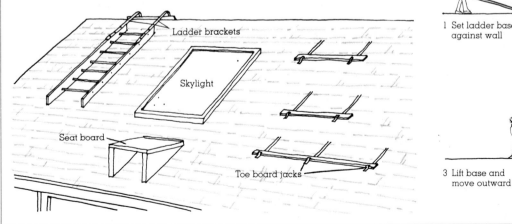

Ladder brackets

Skylight

Seat board

Toe board jacks

1 Set ladder base against wall

2 Walk ladder into upright position

3 Lift base and move outward

4 Base should be away from wall a distance equal to ¼ the ladder's length

. . . Continued from page 102

Step flashing. At the top of the sloping sides of the curb, place step flashing underneath each end of the saddle. Continue to arrange step flashing down the slope, overlapping the pieces at least 2 inches as you slide them under each course of shingles or shakes and under the previous flashing. Again, take care not to puncture the roofing felt.

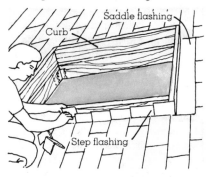

Securing the flashing. Pressing the saddle against the curb, nail the top edge of the saddle to the curb close to the top edge; place nails every 4 to 5 inches. Replace the shingles or shakes, if necessary, over the flange of the saddle and secure them with roofing nails. Cover any exposed nail heads and the surrounding shingles or flashing with a generous amount of roofing cement.

Shoot caulking into the area where the saddle and step flashings overlap. Holding the top edge of the step flashing pieces firmly against the curb, nail them to the curb close to the top edge.

Applying caulking wherever flashings overlap, nail all but the last pieces of step flashing to the curb's sides close to the top edge of the curb. (Standing on step flashing as you nail it down holds it flat against the roof.)

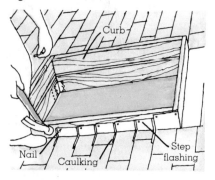

Do not nail down the step flashing to the roof. If shakes or shingles near the edge of the flange are loose, squirt caulking under them and drive a nail through the roofing material; remember to cover nail heads with generous dabs of roofing cement.

Apron flashing. Set the apron, or bottom flashing, down so its sides are under the last pieces of step flashing and its flange rests over the roofing material. Shoot caulking into the area where the last step flashings and the apron overlap; press the step flashings firmly to the roof and nail them to the curb.

Nail the top edge of the apron to the curb. Shoot caulking between the flange of the apron and the shingles or shakes. Nail down the flange of the apron through the roofing material; cover the nail heads and adjoining flashings with a generous dab of roofing cement to prevent leaks through the nail holes.

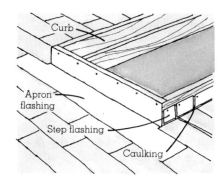

SECURING THE SKYLIGHT

Once you've framed and finished the roof opening, you're ready to secure the skylight. The following methods should work for most models, but it's a good idea to check the directions that accompanied your skylight. If you have the time and the weather is dry, you'll find it easier to build the light shaft (see page 106) before securing the skylight.

Note that preassembled skylights have a layer of paper over the plastic dome to protect against scratches. *Do not* remove this paper until after you've secured the skylight.

Curb-mounted skylight. Run a wavy bead of sealant around the top of the curb; center your skylight over the curb and press it down firmly into the sealant. Nailing through the predrilled holes, secure the skylight's frame to the side of the curb.

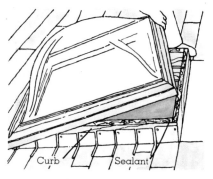

Self-flashing skylight. Set the skylight over the opening and mark the outer edge of the flange on the roof. Remove the skylight and liberally cover the area within the lines with roofing cement.

Next, position the skylight over the opening, making sure all four corners are aligned with the corners of the roof opening. Press the flange firmly into the roofing cement and nail the flange to the roof with roofing nails. Cover the nail heads and the flange with a generous amount of roofing cement (see next page).

If your roof is surfaced with hot-mopped asphalt or with polyurethane foam, you may want a roofing contractor to restore your roof. You can replace shingles or shakes yourself; trim them as necessary to fit against the edge of the curb.

OPENING THE CEILING

After you've secured the skylight, you can cut, frame, and finish the ceiling opening any day, rain or shine. And you can begin enjoying the light streaming in through your skylight even before you've completed framing and finishing the hole in the ceiling.

SECURING A SELF-FLASHING SKYLIGHT

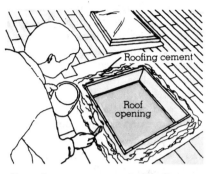

Spread generous amount of roofing cement over area of roof to be covered by skylight flange.

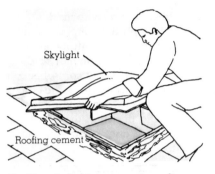

Position skylight over opening, align, and press flange down on roofing cement.

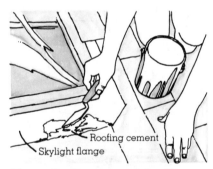

After nailing flange to roof sheathing, cover nail heads and flange with generous amount of roofing cement.

Covering flange, replace shingles and nail to roof. Spread dab of roofing cement over each nail head.

Cutting the ceiling

Since you planned and marked the ceiling opening as the first step in installing your skylight, cutting the opening is fairly straightforward.

Check your markings. Even though you marked the corners and center of the ceiling opening before cutting through the roof, it's a good idea to double-check your markings against both the framed roof opening and the angle of the light shaft.

Check the corner nails and replace any that are missing. Stretch your chalk line around the four nails and snap the line between each pair of nails to mark the opening. Then remove the nails.

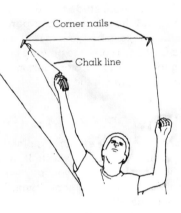

Making the cut. Before you cut the opening, cover the floor and the furniture below with a large tarp and drop cloths. Wear a painter's mask and goggles to protect against the dust while you're cutting. Cut through wallboard (gypsum board) with either a keyhole or reciprocating saw. Cut lath and plaster with a reciprocating saw fitted with a coarse, wood-cutting blade.

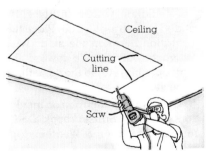

When you come to a joist, cut through only the wallboard to prevent tearing when the ceiling cutout is removed. Ceiling material is quite heavy, so you'll want to cut it out in small pieces if the area of the opening is larger than you can conveniently handle.

After the opening is cut, break off the wallboard and remove the wallboard nails.

Cutting ceiling joists

Before you can cut the ceiling joists, you'll need to reroute any pipes, wiring, or heating or air-conditioning ducts that cross the ceiling opening (see page 70), if you weren't able to plan around them.

If you have to cut one or more joists that are more than 30 inches from a wall, you need to support them before you cut. Using 2 by 4 lumber, cut two pieces long enough to span both the opening and two joists on each side of the opening. Position the pieces at least 12 inches from the edges of the opening, and fasten them with woodscrews to the joists. This will keep the joists from shaking and jiggling when you cut through them, and will prevent nails in the wallboard from popping loose.

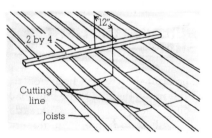

To cut a joist, follow the instructions for cutting a roof rafter (see page 101), with these additional guidelines: if you're planning a straight light shaft, cut the joist at a right angle to the ceiling; mark the angle of cut for an angled or splayed shaft with a straightedge or a length of string positioned between the bottom of the joist and the roof opening. Be sure to allow for the headers by measuring out from the opening.

Framing the ceiling opening

To frame the ceiling opening, refer to the instructions on page 102 for framing the roof opening.

Using joist-hanger nails, nail the hangers to the joists. Set one header into each facing pair of hangers and nail it to the cut end of the joist with 8-penny common nails. Fit the second header into each set of hangers and attach it to the first header with 16-penny common nails driven in in a staggered pattern. Nail the joist hanger flanges to the headers. Repeat on the opposite side of the opening.

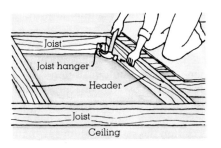

If your ceiling opening doesn't fit exactly between two joists, you'll need to install additional framing members parallel to the joists, along the edge of the opening (see the drawing on page 101).

BUILDING THE LIGHT SHAFT

The light shaft directs light from the skylight on the roof to the interior of your home. The following pages describe how to frame, insulate, and finish a light shaft.

Framing the light shaft

The frame for the light shaft not only provides a nailing surface for the walls, but also joins the ceiling to the roof, giving support to both.

Measure the distance between the ceiling headers and the roof headers at every corner, and at least every 16 inches in between. Cut the vertical studs to the measured lengths.

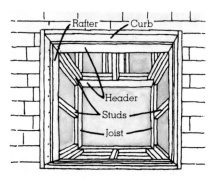

Unless your roof is flat and your light shaft straight, you'll need to cut one or both ends of the studs at an angle.

If you want lights in the shaft (see page 111), position the studs to clear any electrical outlet or recessed light fixtures you plan to install.

Toenail the studs to the ceiling and roof headers with 8-penny nails. Make sure you install two studs at each corner to provide nailing for the wallboard or other material used to finish the shaft.

Insulating the light shaft

For better energy efficiency, plan on insulating the light shaft. If your attic is not insulated, you may want to insulate it at the same time. Be sure to install any electrical wiring before you insulate.

Caution: Remember to wear gloves, a long-sleeved shirt, long pants, a painter's mask, and goggles when working with insulation.

Rolled insulation works best for the short, uneven lengths needed in a light shaft.

Buy 6-inch-thick insulation in the width that will best fit between the studs.

Measure a length of insulation to fit in each stud opening, and cut the insulation with a utility knife guided by a straightedge. Place the insulation between the studs with the vapor-barrier side toward the shaft opening; staple the edge flaps to the studs.

For more information on insulation, see the *Sunset* book *Do-It-Yourself Insulation & Weatherstripping*.

Finishing the light shaft

How you finish the light shaft is limited only by your imagination. Here are some ideas to get you started. Wallboard that is painted white or a light color is one of the best finishes for reflecting light. Finishing with wallboard (see below) and paint is economical, but takes time and skill for good results.

If your walls are paneled, you may want to finish the light shaft to match (see page 108).

Finishing with wallboard. You'll need the following tools and supplies: taping compound, taping knives to apply the compound, and a flat pan to mix it; utility knife to score wallboard; hammer to drive nails; tin snips to cut cornerbead; a rasp to smooth cut wallboard edges; cornerbead or wood molding to trim the ceiling opening; drywall tape; sandpaper; and paint and paint brush or roller.

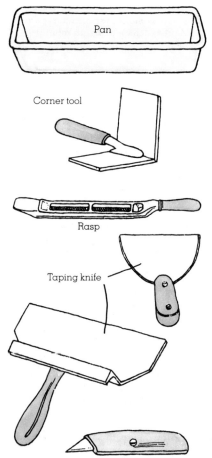

Pan

Corner tool

Rasp

Taping knife

Utility knife

Measuring and cutting.
Measure the cutting lines and angles for each wall of the light shaft; using a straightedge or chalk line, mark the measurements on the wallboard. Place the factory-sealed edge of the wallboard at the top of the wall of the light shaft; that straight, clean edge usually looks better than one you can cut. The cut edge at the bottom will be hidden by a cornerbead or molding.

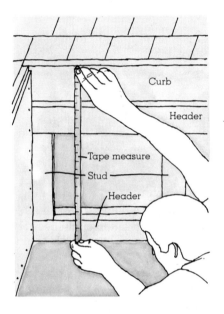

To cut wallboard, score the front paper layer with a utility knife along the cutting line, and break the gypsum core by bending the wallboard to the back. Score the back paper layer along the bend with your utility knife, and snap the board back for a clean break. Smooth rough edges with a rasp.

Installing the wallboard.
To hang wallboard, hold a piece up against the frame of the light shaft, making sure its top and bottom edges are perfectly aligned with the roof and ceiling openings.

Using wallboard nails, fasten the wallboard to the rafters, headers, joists, and studs, spacing nails 6 inches apart. Drive the nails in, dimpling the wallboard surface without puncturing it. Then cover the other sides and the inside of the curb if its sides are angled to the light shaft.

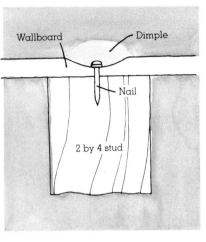

Unless you're trimming the ceiling opening with wood molding, the next step is to nail metal cornerbead to the corners where the ceiling and walls of the light shaft meet.

Measure and cut four cornerbead pieces to length, mitering the ends at 45° angles; use tin snips for cutting. The flanges of the cornerbead form a 90° angle; if you have a splayed or angled light shaft, you'll have to bend the flanges in or out to fit.

Set the cornerbead in place, using wallboard nails to secure both flanges every 6 to 8 inches.

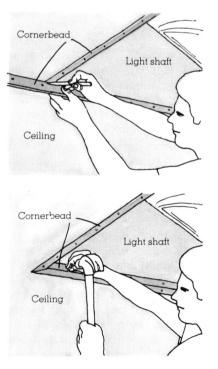

Finishing wallboard. Apply a smooth layer of taping compound to the wallboard on each side of a corner. Measure and tear the drywall tape, fold it in half vertically, and press it into the corner with a corner tool. Apply a thin layer of compound over the tape and smooth it out with the corner tool. Repeat for the remaining corners.

Tape any other joints between panels in a similar manner, except do not fold the tape. Then, using smooth, even strokes with a taping knife, cover the nail dimples with compound unless you're finishing with paneling (see the drawing on the next page).

Allow the taping compound to dry for at least 24 hours. (If it's cold outside, make sure there's heat in the room; otherwise, the compound will shrink and crack.)

If you're installing a light-diffusing or insulating ceiling panel you don't plan to remove often, follow the instructions on page 108. But if you're leaving the light shaft open or putting in a temporary panel, you'll need to finish the light shaft in the following manner.

Lightly sand the compound to get a smooth surface. Check the seams for bubbles; patch them by cross-slitting the bubble with a utility knife, lifting the unglued tape, and applying compound before pressing the tape back into place. Let the patch dry; then sand it smooth.

Using a wide taping knife, apply a second coat of compound over nails and seams, spreading the compound a few inches on each side of the taped seam, feathering the compound out toward the edges.

Let the second coat dry; then sand it and apply a final coat. Use your widest taping knife to smooth out and feather the edges, covering all dimples and seams. After the compound dries, sand it to remove even minor imperfections.

For the final touch, paint the shaft walls in white or a light color for maximum light in the room from the skylight.

TAPING A WALLBOARD JOINT

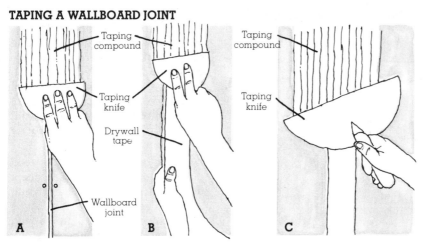

To tape wallboard joint, (A) spread smooth layer of taping compound over joint, (B) bed paper tape into compound, and (C) feathering edges, spread wide layer of compound over tape.

Finishing with paneling. If you choose to finish your light shaft with wood, you can use either plywood or solid board paneling.

The easiest and neatest way of fastening plywood paneling is to secure it to wallboard using adhesive. Tape the joints between the wallboard panels but don't coat the nail heads.

Solid board paneling can be purchased in several species of wood and a variety of edge treatments—square edge, tongue-and-groove, or shiplap, among others. You may find some prefinished board paneling, particularly floor boards, that can be used on walls. Solid board panels can be applied to the walls of your light shaft horizontally, vertically, or diagonally. Solid board paneling can be fastened with adhesive or nailed.

For more on choosing and installing plywood and board paneling, see the *Sunset* book *Paneling, Papering & Wallpapering.*

Installing plywood panels. Measure the light shaft for plywood paneling in the same way as for wallboard (see page 107).

Using a fine-tooth saw (10 to 15 teeth per inch), cut the plywood panels—face up with a handsaw or table saw, face down with a portable circular saw or saber saw. If the finished face tends to splinter as you cut, cover the cutting line with

masking tape or score it with a knife. If you're cutting paneling from the back, remember to draw the outline in mirror image—the reverse of how you want the front to look. Cut the edges of the panels at a slight angle (about 5°) to make them easier to fit into place. Slope the angle inward toward the back of the panel.

When applying panels with adhesive, follow the manufacturers' instructions for both the paneling and the adhesive. Work with only one panel at a time—don't apply adhesive beyond the area the panel will cover.

Installing solid board panels. Each piece of solid board paneling must be measured separately and then cut. If an end is to be cut at an angle, set a sliding T-bevel to the proper angle.

Using a fine-tooth saw (10 to 15 teeth per inch), cut the boards—finished face up with a handsaw or table saw, face down with a portable circular saw or saber saw.

Though you can fasten board panels to the walls of the light shaft with nails, adhesive works better. The light shaft receives a lot of solar heat; securing the boards with adhesive prevents them from warping, twisting, or cupping. To apply the adhesive and install the boards, follow the directions for plywood panels (see above), except apply a

squiggly line of adhesive to the wall under each board.

Trimming the light shaft. Apply molding around the ceiling opening, being sure the molding is wide enough to cover the edges of the paneling and the wallboard, as well as the joint between the wallboard and the ceiling. Miter the corners. Use either casing or corner molding.

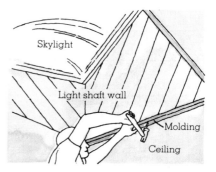

Unless you accurately fit the paneling in the corners of the light shaft, you'll want to apply quarter-round molding to finish these corners.

Either nail the molding in place with finishing nails or use panel adhesive. Be careful not to smear adhesive on the exposed surfaces of the paneling.

INSTALLING A CEILING PANEL

Ceiling panels can be clear or translucent, temporary or permanent. They can add insulative value to your skylight and, when translucent, help distribute the light evenly.

Some skylight manufacturers make ceiling panels and provide the hardware for installing them. Almost all panels are made from plastic. You can buy an acrylic, polycarbonate, or other plastic panel (see page 21) cut to size from a store that sells plastics. Building departments seldom approve the use of glass for diffusing panels in homes because of the risks involved if they shatter.

Plastic sheets are commonly available in thicknesses ranging from ⅛ inch to ½ inch. Plastic tends to sag with time; you'll probably have to install cross supports under the panel (check your local building codes and the manufacturer's recommendations).

To install a panel you plan to leave in place, trim the opening with wood molding and slide the panel into place.

Miter the corners of the molding and secure the molding so the lip extends ½ inch around the inside of the opening. To measure the opening for the panel, subtract ¼ inch from both the length and the width to ease fitting the panel into place. Holding the panel at a slight angle, lift it into the opening; then set it on the lip of the molding.

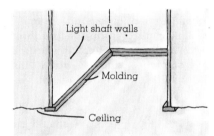

Wood molding also works well for an insulating panel (see page 29) which you want to remove from time to time. To remove the panel, all you need to do is push up from below, turn it to a slight angle, and lift it out.

INSTALLING A SKYLIGHT IN AN OPEN-BEAM CEILING

Installing a skylight in an open-beam ceiling is easier and takes much less time than working with a finished ceiling, since you don't have to cut a hole in the ceiling and build a light shaft. Consider the spacing between the rafters when choosing the size of the skylight to minimize the framing you'll need to do (see page 99).

Using the list on page 96, assemble the tools and supplies that apply to open-beam construction. You'd also be wise to read through the installation instructions on pages 98–104; though many of the directions are only for homes with finished ceilings, you will need to refer to that section as you work.

Determining the dimensions of the opening

In open-beam construction, the curb on which the skylight rests may sit on a framed opening (see page 102) or can fit inside the roof opening as described below. For the curb to fit inside the opening, you'll need to know the *outside* dimensions of the curb; then you can cut your opening to that size.

If the manufacturer doesn't provide the curb's outside dimensions, compute them by adding twice the curb's thickness to the length and width of the manufacturers' recommended dimensions for the roof opening.

Planning the opening

Decide where you want to position your skylight (see page 17). Measure and mark on the ceiling the corners of the opening. Drill a hole at each corner and drive a 16-penny nail through each hole to mark the opening on the roof. If any wiring (usually it's exposed) crosses the marked opening, see page 70 for information on rerouting it.

Building a curb

Whether you're using a self-flashing or a curb-mounted skylight, follow the instructions on page 100 to build a curb for your skylight. Be sure to use lumber wide enough to reach from the ceiling to the top of the roof sheathing for a self-flashing skylight, or from the ceiling to the required height above the roof for a curb-mounted skylight.

If you're planning to finish the ceiling opening with molding, you don't need to brace the curb to keep it square; instead, cut the molding and nail it to the curb's bottom edge (the edge that faces the room below). Buy molding wide enough to hide the bottom edge of the curb, as well as the joint between the curb and the ceiling. Measure and cut the molding to fit ¼ to ½ inch in from the curb's inside edge, mitering the corners for a perfect fit. Using finishing nails, nail the molding to the curb; drive the nails below the wood surface with a nailset, and cover the nail holes with wood putty.

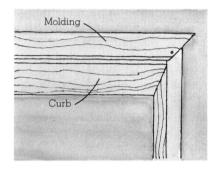

Opening the roof

You plan and cut the roof opening for open-beam construction in much the same way as finished-ceiling construction, with two differences. First, you don't need to carry the curb to the roof to outline the opening; simply mark the opening by marking lines between the nails with your chalk line.

Second, you don't have to frame the opening unless you need to cut rafters; the curb, which extends from the outside to the inside of the roof, serves the same purpose. If you do have to cut one or more rafters, frame the opening as described on page 102, except you'll nail through the rafters and into the headers instead of using unattractive joist hangers. The curb should then extend to the bottom of the rafters.

Keep these exceptions in mind as you prepare, outline, and cut the roof opening following the instructions on pages 100–101.

To check the opening's squareness, measure diagonally from corner to corner; the distances should be identical.

Installing and flashing the curb

In open-beam construction, install the curb from the *underside* of the roof instead of setting it over the roof opening as with finished-ceiling construction. Unless you're using a self-flashing skylight, you flash the curb in exactly the same way for both types of construction (see page 102).

With a helper, lift the curb up to the ceiling and fit it inside the roof opening. The molding should fit tightly against the ceiling or against the framing if you cut a rafter (see above). While your helper holds the curb in place, nail it to the rafters and headers every 6 inches with 8-penny finishing nails.

Drive the nails below the wood surface with a nailset, and cover the holes with wood putty. Then finish the flashing.

Securing the skylight

Follow the directions on page 104 to set your skylight over the curb. The paper over the plastic dome of a preassembled skylight protects the dome from scratches. *Do not* remove the paper until you've positioned the skylight.

TAKING CARE OF YOUR SKYLIGHT

Once they're installed, skylights require only a minimum of maintenance and cleaning. Because of their shape, slope, and location, heavy rains wash away most of the dirt. Occasionally, you'll need to clean the inside—and the outside, too, if rain doesn't do the job.

Caring for the frame

Most skylight frames are made of aluminum (colored ones are anodized) and require no care other than washing when you clean the skylight glazing. If you live by the ocean where the salt from spray can eat into aluminum, you'll have to protect the frame with paint. If your skylight frame has a painted metal finish, check it annually, touching up any bare spots with a paint recommended by the manufacturer.

Protecting and preserving plastic

Acrylic and polycarbonate are the two types of plastic generally used in skylights. The cleaning and repair suggestions below apply to acrylic and, for the most part, to polycarbonate.

If your skylight is made from fiberglass, follow the manufacturer's instructions for proper care of the glazing.

Cleaning plastics. Plastic glazing is susceptible to scratches and abrasions, as well as to damage by certain solvents. You'll want to observe some general precautions when cleaning a plastic skylight:

• Never use abrasive cleansers, abrasive pads, or gritty cloths.

• Do not remove dirt by scraping with a sharp tool, such as a razor blade or putty knife.

• Do not clean with window-cleaning fluids or strong solvents such as gasoline, denatured alcohol, carbon tetrachloride, or acetone. They will cause the plastic to craze with minute cracks.

To clean a plastic skylight, use either a solution of mild soap or detergent and water or a weak solution of household ammonia and water (*do not* use ammonia for polycarbonates). Apply with a soft cloth or cellulose sponge and rinse well with clear water. To prevent water spots, blot dry with a chamois or a damp cellulose sponge.

To remove foreign material (protective paper, glazing compound, caulking, roofing tar, grease, or fresh oil paint) from acrylic, use hexane, a good grade of naptha, kerosene, or methanol applied with a soft cloth. Use a good grade of naptha, isopropyl alcohol, or butyl cellosolve on polycarbonate domes. Then clean the skylight as described above.

Protecting plastic. To maintain the luster of plastic, protect it with a thin, even coat of automobile polish (*not* cleaner polish) or floor or automobile wax applied with a clean, soft cloth. Buff lightly and wipe with a clean, damp cloth to remove static electricity, which attracts dirt.

Plastic repair. You can minimize or remove minor scratches and abrasions from plastic, and often control cracks.

Minor scratches and abrasions can sometimes be obscured with automobile wax applied as described above. If this method doesn't work, try polishing the scratched area of the plastic with a good grade of automobile cleaner-polish on a soft cloth. The fine abrasive in the cleaner-polish smooths the scratches, and the wax in the polish fills them, reducing their visibility.

Major scratches should be repaired by a knowledgeable professional.

Cracks can be kept from lengthening—drill a ⅛-inch-diameter hole at each end of the crack and fill the holes with silicone sealant.

Looking after glass

You can clean clear or coated glass either with commercial glass-cleaning solutions or with a weak solution of household ammonia, mild soap, or detergent (if rinsed thoroughly) and water. Apply with a sponge and dry with paper towels, a chamois, or, if the glass is flat, a squeegee.

To prevent scratches, abrasions, and deterioration, *never* clean coated, sun-control glass with abrasive cleansers, gritty sponges, or metal objects such as razor blades or putty knives.

Even after the sun goes down, you can approximate the daytime effects of changing seasons and weather conditions by installing lights in your skylight's light shaft and controlling them with a dimmer switch on the wall. A diffusing panel mounted below the skylight at ceiling height hides the fixtures and spreads the light evenly.

Illuminating the light shaft

If you don't mind cutting through your walls, you can add lights to your light shaft and a dimmer switch to your wall any time you wish. But in a light shaft under construction, the time to install the wiring is after the shaft has been framed and before it's closed in with wallboard or paneling.

For instructions on installing lighting, see the *Sunset* book *Basic Home Wiring Illustrated*. The light bulbs you choose and the type of dimmer you use to control them depend on the amount and kind of light you want.

Fluorescents vs. incandescents. Though more expensive than incandescent bulbs, fluorescents are cooler and more energy-efficient where long-term artificial light is needed. They give three times more light per watt than incandescent bulbs and last 15 times longer. Ranging from 6 to 60 watts, fluorescent tubes are available in straight and doughnut shapes (the latter is ideal for illuminating a light shaft evenly from one fixture) and in a variety of shades. The tubes sold as "full spectrum" most closely simulate sunlight.

Incandescent bulbs are easier to connect to most dimmer switches than fluorescents, and offer greater wattage. Standard incandescents range from 15 to 300 watts and have an average life of 1,000 hours, though you can buy bulbs that last for 2,500 hours.

Incandescent tubes distribute light more evenly than bulbs, but require special sockets for installation. Ranging from 25 to 100 watts, they have an average life of 1,000 hours.

Be sure to place all incandescent bulbs and tubes at least 6 inches from the diffusing panel or surrounding building material; otherwise, the heat build-up can get dangerously high.

Whatever type of bulb you use (the doughnut shape excepted), mount two or more bulbs at equal intervals around the light shaft to minimize shadows below.

Choosing a dimmer switch. With a continuous dimmer, you turn the knob or move a lever to vary illumination from none to full brightness. Dimmers for both incandescent and fluorescent bulbs have different power capacities—up to 600, 1,000, or 2,000 watts.

Another type is the touch-plate dimmer, designed for incandescents only. It has no moving parts, but reacts to the heat of your body. A brief touch turns lights on or off; the amount of time you leave your finger on the wall plate determines how brightly or dimly the lights glow.

New on the market is a relatively expensive solid-state electronic dimmer for fluorescent bulbs only. You can wire it to fixtures without having to install a dimmer "ballast" that operates a fluorescent tube at its proper electrical rating when using a conventional dimmer. One model has a power capacity of up to 2,000 watts.

It's easy to replace ordinary switches with dimmer switches; many dimmers fit inside standard switch boxes.

Spreading light with a diffusing panel

A diffusing panel, a translucent panel at ceiling height, can be added to an existing light shaft or installed at the time the light shaft is being constructed. See page 108 for instructions on installing a ceiling panel.

Mounting the unit so it can be removed easily allows you to take it down for washing and leave it off for a view of the sky (if the skylight above is clear).

Most diffusing panels are translucent acrylic, polycarbonate, or other plastic (see page 21). Not only is the plastic nearly unbreakable, it's also extremely lightweight—from 3 to 10 ounces per square foot. Depending on the size and thickness, you may have to provide support for the panel to prevent sagging. Check with your supplier or building department.

A glass diffusing panel is heavy, expensive, and breakable; most building departments prohibit the use of glass in homes.

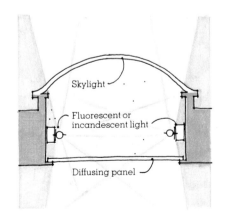

Skylight

Fluorescent or incandescent light

Diffusing panel

INDEX

Boldface numbers refer to color photographs